SHAPING THE
MODERN
DISCIPLE
Lessons from Jesus's Apostles

A DEVOTIONAL FROM
THE BIBLE-TEACHING MINISTRY OF
CHARLES R. SWINDOLL

SHAPING THE MODERN DISCIPLE
Lessons from Jesus's Apostles

From the Bible-Teaching Ministry of Charles R. Swindoll

Charles R. Swindoll has devoted his life to the accurate, practical teaching and application of God's Word and His grace. A pastor at heart, Chuck has served as senior pastor to congregations in Texas, Massachusetts, and California. Since 1998, he has served as the founder and senior pastor-teacher of Stonebriar Community Church in Frisco, Texas, but Chuck's listening audience extends far beyond a local church body. As a leading program in Christian broadcasting since 1979, *Insight for Living* airs in major Christian radio markets around the world, reaching people groups in languages they can understand. Chuck's extensive writing ministry has also served the body of Christ worldwide and his leadership as president and now chancellor of Dallas Theological Seminary has helped prepare and equip a new generation for ministry. Chuck and Cynthia, his partner in life and ministry, have four grown children, ten grandchildren, and two great-grandchildren.

Published By
IFL Publishing House
A Division of Insight for Living Ministries
Post Office Box 1050
Frisco, Texas 75034-0018

Editor in Chief: Cynthia Swindoll, President, Insight for Living Ministries
Executive Vice President: Wayne Stiles, Th.M., D.Min., Dallas Theological Seminary
Writers: John Adair, Th.M., Ph.D., Dallas Theological Seminary
  Malia Rodriguez, Th.M., Dallas Theological Seminary
  Wayne Stiles, Th.M., D.Min., Dallas Theological Seminary
Content Editor: Kathryn Robertson, M.A., English, Hardin-Simmons University
Copy Editors: Jim Craft, M.A., English, Mississippi College
  Paula McCoy, B.A., English, Texas A&M University-Commerce
Project Coordinator, Creative Ministries: Megan Meckstroth, B.S., Advertising, University of Florida
Project Coordinator, Publishing: Melissa Cleghorn, B.A., University of North Texas
Proofreader: LeeAnna Smith, B.A., Communications, Moody Bible Institute
Designer: Margaret Gulliford, B.A., Graphic Design, Taylor University
Production Artist: Nancy Gustine, B.F.A., Advertising Art, University of North Texas

ISBN: 978-1-62655-015-5
Printed in the United States of America

TABLE OF CONTENTS

ABOUT THE WRITERS

JOHN ADAIR
Th.M., Ph.D., Dallas Theological Seminary

John received his master of theology degree in Historical Theology from Dallas Theological Seminary, where he also completed his Ph.D. in Theological Studies. He serves as a writer in the Creative Ministries Department of Insight for Living Ministries. John, his wife, Laura, and their three children reside in Frisco, Texas.

MALIA RODRIGUEZ
Th.M., Dallas Theological Seminary

Malia received her master of theology degree in Systematic Theology from Dallas Theological Seminary. She now serves as a writer in the Creative Ministries Department of Insight for Living Ministries, where she is able to merge her love of theology with her gift for words. Malia and her husband, Matt, who is also a graduate of Dallas Theological Seminary, live in the Dallas area with their son.

WAYNE STILES
Th.M., D.Min., Dallas Theological Seminary

Wayne received his master of theology in Pastoral Ministries and doctor of ministry in Biblical Geography from Dallas Theological Seminary. In 2005, after serving in the pastorate for fourteen years, Wayne joined the staff at Insight for Living Ministries, where he leads and labors alongside a team of writers, editors, and pastors as the executive vice president and chief content officer. Wayne and his wife, Cathy, live in Aubrey, Texas, and have two daughters in college.

A NOTE FROM CHUCK SWINDOLL

The disciples of Jesus were a motley crew. Yes, they were handpicked by the Messiah. And sure, they dropped their nets and other pursuits to follow Him. But they carried with them visions of grandeur. They argued over who was "the greatest." They kept forgetting their lessons. They trembled in their sandals while the Creator slept by their sides. And at the Lord's greatest moment of need, they fled. One of them even betrayed Him.

What lessons can we learn about discipleship from this ragged bunch? How did Jesus take these men—with all their faults—and make them the foundation of the two thousand-year-old enterprise we call the church? What did He employ to train them?

The curriculum of association.

Jesus didn't set up a school. He didn't begin a seminary. He didn't assign to them a well-outlined course of study. He didn't even introduce them through a membership class. He offered them no security, no retirement plan, no list of regulations for them to sign to become His followers. In *Him* they discovered all the schooling they needed. Jesus trained them through personal contact . . . and His training was continuous.

We can see in the lives of these men four general truths about discipleship. First, association with Jesus has threatening moments. How would the disciples react when their safety was threatened? They couldn't calm the sea—and the sea proved one of their smaller threats! They also couldn't deny their inclination to fail. Associating with Jesus means having that inclination exposed. To be disciples, we have to open ourselves to threatening moments.

Second, association with Jesus calls for sacrifice. The disciples had to sacrifice their time. When He called, they dropped their work and followed. They also had to sacrifice their privacy, living in close quarters for three years and being watched daily by followers and skeptics. Eventually, the disciples gave up their lives. To be disciples, sacrifice is a given.

Third, association with Jesus requires total honesty. We all live with a certain amount of fear, especially of what others might think if they really knew us. Yet, discipleship insists we join others in following Jesus. We can't do this without honesty. (And more often than not, when we show the cracks in our lives, others feel closer to us, not further away.)

Finally, association with Jesus tests our love and loyalty. Jesus loved His followers. He was loyal to them to the very end. And He expected the same from them. Throughout the Lord's ministry, at the cross, and after the ascension, the disciples found their love and their loyalty tested again and again. Living as a disciple in His image today prompts us to show love and loyalty to our Lord . . . and to others.

The path of the disciple is a demanding road. We see that in these general truths about association with Jesus. The stories you'll find in this book will give you the specifics of how those who were chosen as special messengers of the gospel by Jesus Himself went on to pass, or fail, the test. As you read, I hope you will be encouraged to follow more faithfully and to love more consistently as the Lord molds *you* into His true disciple.

Charles R. Swindoll

SHAPING THE
MODERN
DISCIPLE

Lessons from Jesus's Apostles

JOHN
EQUIPPED TO LOVE

If we love one another, God abides in us,
and His love is perfected in us.
—1 John 4:12

JOHN

■ MEANING OF NAME
The name John means "Yahweh is a gracious giver."

■ VOCATION
Fisherman, along with his brother, James; partners with Peter and Andrew

■ ORIGIN
Galilee

■ WHEN CALLED BY CHRIST
Early in Jesus's ministry

■ DEATH
Likely died of natural causes in Ephesus around AD 100

■ GEOGRAPHY OF MINISTRY
Jerusalem to Ephesus

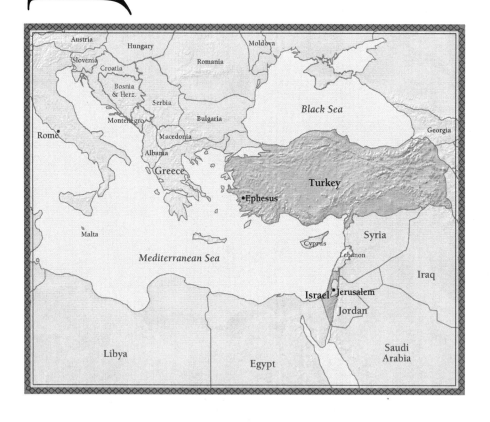

Growing up along the northern edge of Galilee's sea, young John had known the world as a small, predictable place. Born to a family of fishermen, John had learned to make his living casting nets, pushing oars, and gutting fish. The routine work of a first-century fisherman had kept the young man close to home. And although the presence of Romans in Capernaum (the largest city in the vicinity) would have given John plenty of opportunity to do business with a wide variety of people, John's Jewish faith would have ensured that his inner circle didn't stretch beyond bloodlines and the local synagogue.

When Jesus called John and his brother James, along with their colleagues Peter and Andrew, they dropped their nets immediately and took their first steps into a world much wider than they could've imagined. In this new world, John's old ways of thinking and acting would have to pass away, if he wanted to become a true follower of Jesus.

And twice Jesus confronted John's old ways. In the first, the ex-fisherman attempted to show his faithfulness to Christ's righteousness by recounting a story involving a man outside their small band of disciples who was going around casting out demons in Jesus's name (Luke 9:49). John, troubled by the scene, rushed to stop the man. This, John told the Lord, was because the man wasn't part of the group of disciples who followed Jesus day after day.

The Lord's response had to have stunned John: "Do not hinder him; for he who is not against you is for you" (9:50). John had immediately rejected the man because he was an outsider, but Jesus took an optimistic tack. Though the man wasn't under Jesus's daily teaching, he worked in Jesus's name and, therefore, was presumably a faithful follower. With one statement, Jesus shot down John's desire to keep fellow believers out of ministry simply because they weren't part of His group. Later, as Jesus and His disciples moved toward Jerusalem, the Lord took this lesson even further.

As the group journeyed, Jesus sent a few disciples ahead to make arrangements for Him to stay in a Samaritan village (9:51–52). The Jews and the Samaritans had long been at odds. The rupture went all the way back to the divided northern and southern kingdoms of Israel and Judah in the Old Testament, but in the centuries just prior to the New Testament era, Jewish-Samaritan animosity had flared. The heat had risen when the Samaritans took sides against the Jews in the Maccabean wars. Then, Jewish leader John

Hyrcanus led a group to destroy the Samaritan temple in the late second century BC. These hostilities had led Jews and Samaritans to treat each other with avoidance and suspicion.

That Jesus sent His disciples into a Samaritan village indicates that the Lord was not at all interested in this "policy" of avoidance and suspicion. However, the Samaritans rejected the messengers Jesus sent because His final destination was Jerusalem—a rival center of worship to that of the Samaritans. While Scripture doesn't make it explicit, this rejection no doubt pleased some of the Jews traveling with Jesus who had been suspicious about staying in an "enemy" village anyway.

John and his brother James reacted to the Samaritans' rejection with righteous indignation, suggesting to Jesus that they command fire from heaven to consume the village (Luke 9:54). Putting aside the amusing notion that John and James could have actually commanded fire from heaven, their response reveals once again the easy dismissiveness John held toward those outside the "approved" group. Indeed, this was such a deep-seated feeling in the disciple that he was ready to kill innocent villagers. John's old ways couldn't have been more apparent. Jesus, in return, appropriately rebuked the brothers for their thoughtlessness.

John's attitude reminds us that Jesus didn't choose finished products to be His disciples. He chose men who needed refining, who needed their hard edges shorn off. And by the end of Jesus's ministry on earth, John's narrow view of the world had expanded. In fact, love for others became a key quality in John's ministry and in his writings.

We see the first hints of this change in John's gospel, where he portrayed himself as the disciple that Jesus loved, the one who reclined on the Lord during the Last Supper (John 13:23). John also reported that he witnessed the crucifixion alongside Jesus's mother, Mary, and that in that moment, the Lord called upon John to care for Mary as his own mother (19:26–27). Jesus knew John had changed. The love the Lord had lavished upon the disciple had produced its desired effect: love begat love.

As a follower of Christ, John came to understand the importance of reaching out to others in love—a stark contrast from his fire-casting days. The best evidence for John's new commitment comes in his epistles, which explicitly teach the importance of loving one another. The love of Christ in the crucifixion set the path for His disciples, according to John (1 John 3:16). Where John once sought to spread fear in those outside Jesus's small band of disciples, he later taught that "there is no fear in love; but perfect love casts out fear, because fear involves punishment, and the one who fears is not perfected in love" (4:18).

John's world expanded because of his time spent with Jesus. No longer did the disciple seek to oppress outsiders with fearful pronouncements. John knew judgment would come in the future, but it wasn't his to give. Jesus showed him that making people afraid was not the way to get them to see God's love and be led to true repentance. Therefore, John exhorted Jesus's followers to walk in the spirit of the Lord's great commandment—love one another. Only in this will we embody the kind of inviting grace that Jesus faithfully gave and regularly affirmed.

—John Adair

The Rest of the Story: Luke 9:46–56; 1 John 3–4

TAKE IT TO HEART

Why do you think Jesus responded to outsiders the way He did? How can you better relate to "outsiders" in your community?

_____

_____

_____

_____

_____

_____

_____

_____

ANDREW
A GOOD CATCH

[Andrew] found first his own brother Simon and said to him, "We have found the Messiah."
—John 1:41

ANDREW

■ **MEANING OF NAME**
Andrew derives from the Greek word *Andreas* meaning "manly."

■ **VOCATION**
Fisherman

■ **ORIGIN**
Bethsaida

■ **WHEN CALLED BY CHRIST**
While fishing (Matthew 4:18–19)

■ **GEOGRAPHY OF MINISTRY AND DEATH**
"He preached the gospel to many Asiatic nations; but on his arrival at Edessa [southeastern Turkey] he was taken and crucified on a cross, the two ends of which were fixed transversely in the ground. Hence the derivation of the term, St. Andrew's Cross." [1]

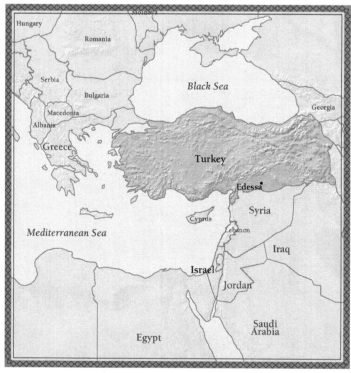

Day in and day out, Andrew toiled alongside his brother Simon, casting nets and dragging them in full of fish. At the end of each day, the fisherman must have felt physically fatigued yet satisfied with his work. But as Andrew lay down his head, his body aching from a hard day of labor, his soul must've also ached. Though he had found success in his vocation, something was missing.

So Andrew searched.

Each day, Andrew put one sandaled foot before the other. Maybe one day soon God would give him the peace he longed for. Surely the dusty path that stretched out before him led to solace—he just had to keep looking.

Then one day Andrew met a man like no one he had ever known. The man wore strange clothes, survived on a diet of bugs and honey, and lived as a recluse on the outskirts of society (Mark 1:6). But as Andrew listened, this man spoke of life and forgiveness and hope. Andrew knew John the Baptist's words were true—he had come from God.

Andrew believed the baptisms John performed were preparing his small group of followers for something new. Andrew's hope began to grow. As John spoke to his followers, he reminded them that although they lived in a dark world where sin, legalism, and oppressive powers reigned, the Light was coming. Recognizing the greatness and holiness of John the Baptist, Andrew must have struggled to imagine how someone could be greater. But John insisted he himself was not the Light. One was coming who would give light, grace, and truth to all who would believe in Him (John 1:6–9, 14).

Later, as Andrew walked with John the Baptist in Bethany, a man passed by whom Andrew didn't recognize. All of a sudden, John yelled, "Behold, the Lamb of God!" (1:36) and pointed to Jesus, the sacrificial Lamb of God who would give Andrew the peace he had searched for.

So Andrew followed (1:37).

After spending the day with Jesus, Andrew immediately found his brother Simon and brought him to Jesus. "We have found the Messiah" (1:41). Having found rest for his soul, Andrew wanted his brother to find the same peace . . . and not only his brother but as many as God would bring into the new disciple's path.

9

After spending the day with Jesus, Andrew likely shared with Simon all that Jesus had said and done. And when Andrew woke up the next morning and went to work, he must have done so with new energy and excitement . . . a whole new outlook on life. Surely, he wondered when he would see Jesus again and hoped it would be soon.

Then one day as Andrew and Simon fished on the Sea of Galilee, Jesus called to them from the shore: "Follow Me, and I will make you become fishers of men" (Mark 1:17). Andrew and Simon dropped their nets at once, abandoned their trade, and obeyed Jesus. They became His permanent disciples and later members of His chosen twelve apostles (Luke 6:13). These men followed His call to commit themselves to catching men and women and bringing them to Jesus.

We know of a few people Andrew brought to Jesus but perhaps none as memorable as one little boy out of a crowd of five thousand. After healing a lame man and condemning the Pharisees because they judged Him for performing miracles on the Sabbath rather than believing in Him as their Messiah, Jesus and His apostles crossed to the far side of the Sea of Galilee. A huge crowd followed. As thousands of people filled the hillside, Jesus asked Philip, "Where are we to buy bread, so that these may eat?" (John 6:5). When Philip didn't have the answer, Andrew spoke up and brought a little boy and his lunch to Jesus.

But uncertainty dampened Andrew's faith (6:9). After watching Jesus turn water into wine, clear the temple of evil merchants, heal a young boy, and make a lame man walk, Andrew should've known Jesus could do something with five loaves of bread and two small fish. Perhaps part of him did. After walking with the Messiah, watching Him work, and listening to His words, Andrew had enough faith to bring the boy to Jesus. But then the apostle wondered out loud what good such a small amount of food could do for over five thousand people. Andrew still had a life-changing lesson to learn: all he had to do was bring to Jesus the resources he had and watch as Jesus multiplied them to meet the people's needs.

Andrew didn't have all the answers. He didn't know how a little bread and fish could feed thousands of people, but he knew his Lord could do miraculous things. This apostle's life reminds us to trust the Lord to meet our needs and remember that the Creator of the universe will equip us for the good works He has prepared for us. If the Lord gives us a seemingly impossible task, we must bring to Him our insufficiency and watch as He turns it into enough. Andrew learned that lesson early on and began to trust Jesus daily. Then this fisherman who searched for and found Jesus started searching for others to bring to Him. Andrew knew that Jesus would meet their needs, too. The apostle appears only a few times in the Gospels, but each time, he is bringing someone to Jesus (John 1:41; 6:9; 12:22).

Andrew's faith should encourage us to bring to Jesus both the people we know who seem beyond redemption and the trials we face that don't seem to have solutions. As we do, we will learn to trust God's sovereign provision in our lives. And most certainly, our Lord will teach us to trust Him as He transforms us through trials and leads us into victory.

—*Malia Rodriguez*

The Rest of the Story: John 6

TAKE IT TO HEART

What people played a part in bringing you to Jesus? Who has God placed in your life whom you can bring to Jesus?

PETER

HUMBLED FOR SACRIFICE

Simon Peter answered, "You are the Christ,
the Son of the living God."
—Matthew 16:16

PETER

■ MEANING OF NAME
Simon means "hearer," while Peter means "rock."

■ VOCATION
Fisherman, along with his brother, Andrew; partners with James and John

■ ORIGIN
Galilee

■ WHEN CALLED BY CHRIST
Early in Jesus's ministry

■ DEATH
Crucified upside down, probably in AD 66–68

■ GEOGRAPHY OF MINISTRY
From Israel to Rome

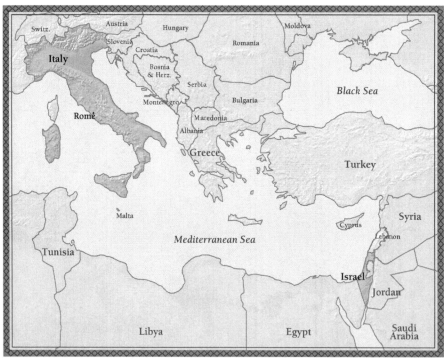

U pon the fruitful waters of the Sea of Galilee, the waves splashed softly against the hull of Simon Peter's fishing boat as the tensile net reached its breaking point. After catching nothing all day, Jesus had told Peter and his brother Andrew to lower their nets one final time. The bounty of fish that flooded in was too heavy. The two hearty fishermen were forced to call over the sons of Zebedee, James and John, just to bring the catch onto the boat. Finished loading the fish, Peter dropped to his knees among the lithe, shining bodies flapping out their last breaths and said, "Go away from me Lord, for I am a sinful man" (Luke 5:8).

Humbled and terrified by the generosity and power of Jesus, Peter sensed his own unworthiness and thought it best they separate. Jesus thought just the opposite and invited Peter to put aside his fear and learn to fish for people (Matthew 4:19; Luke 5:10). For the better part of the next three years, Peter followed Jesus. During that time, the fisherman witnessed Jesus perform miracles, heal the sick, and teach the masses. The disciple grew under Jesus's ministry, peaking as the group journeyed far north to the region around Caesarea Philippi, located in the shadow of Mount Hermon.

This location would have been considered remote to most first-century Jews. Pagan worshipers populated the city and surrounding areas. A prominent shrine to Pan, the Greek god of shepherds and flocks, sat just outside the city. In the region of this place dedicated to the worship of a false god and a false shepherd, Jesus—the true God and the Good Shepherd—presented to Peter one of the most decisive questions he would ever encounter: "But who do you say that I am?" (Matthew 16:15). Peter answered, "You are the Christ, the Son of the living God" (16:16).

In one glorious moment, Peter spoke, for the first time, those words that changed the course of human history. From there, the apostle would take this confession to his own people and also to the Gentile pagans who lived outside the borders of Israel.

But God chooses broken people—those who need Him—to accomplish His work in the world. Peter's brokenness was hard to miss. Immediately following this exchange, the apostle had another with Jesus in which the Good Shepherd predicted His suffering and death (16:21; John 10:11, 14–15). Peter, zealous to minister alongside and in service to the Son of God, felt his temperature rising. He pulled Jesus aside and rebuked the Lord for suggesting such a devastating course of action.

Peter was humble before the Lord—even willing to die for Him (John 13:37)—but the apostle struggled to accept the humiliation Jesus would suffer on the cross. He had not yet learned one of the most significant lessons for those who want to follow Jesus: the Shepherd humbles Himself for His sheep. Peter's humility allowed him to give his own life for the Lord. But his pride would not allow him to accept Jesus's giving His life for those beneath Him. Indeed, Jesus called Peter's prideful mentality *satanic*, responding with, "Get behind Me, Satan!" (Matthew 16:23).

Peter is such an everyman. One minute he's relishing in his moment of triumph, and the next he's buried under the weight of his prideful shortsightedness. But Peter resembles us in another way.

Peter had no problem affirming the true identity of Jesus. Words are easy . . . they always have been. This doesn't diminish Peter's confession, which was certainly remarkable. But when we place that confession in the context of Peter's response to the actions required to live up to Jesus's standard of humility, suddenly the disciple looks very familiar. Like most of us, letting words out of his mouth came to Peter easily. But things quickly got a lot more difficult. When it came time for Jesus to give His life for the poor, the weak, and the hungry, Peter would have none of it.

Later, Peter's struggle continued as he resisted Jesus's humble offer to wash his feet (John 13:8). And then, perhaps most famously, Peter denied Christ three times the night the Lord was arrested (18:17, 25–27). His earlier confession seemed to crumble. These incidents reflect Peter's challenge to identify fully with the humbling and self-giving work of Jesus on the cross. Even Peter, one of the closest to Jesus during the Lord's ministry, had this struggle. How much more so for us?

After the resurrection, Peter found himself once again fishing in the soft splash of Galilee's waves. Once again Peter had just returned from a night without a catch. And once again, Peter heard a call to cast his nets one more time (21:6).

Peter didn't recognize the man on the beach who had called to him, but he listened. And this time, the catch was even more abundant than before, so the apostles fishing with Peter had to help drag the net onto land, where they found the resurrected Jesus tending a fire. After a breakfast of freshly grilled fish, Peter spoke with the Lord one more time in the place where it all began.

Jesus asked Peter three times whether he loved Him. Each time, Peter answered yes. And each time, Jesus gave a similar reply: "Tend My lambs," "Shepherd My sheep," and "Tend My sheep" (John 21:15–17). Peter had readily affirmed the person of Jesus in Caesarea Philippi, but he struggled to affirm the Lord's purpose on earth: Jesus's humble sacrifice. That struggle haunted the disciple up to and through the resurrection. Only there, back on the beach in Galilee with the resurrected Jesus before him, did Peter finally receive the command Jesus had intended for him all along. Now he—and the other apostles—could carry Jesus's teaching to the ends of the earth. And carry it on Peter did, all the way to his own crucifixion some thirty years later.

—John Adair

The Rest of the Story: Acts 2–4

TAKE IT TO HEART

How have you struggled with living a humbled and sacrificial life? What can you do to better take up Christ's cause, as Peter did after Christ's ascension?

PHILIP

BECOMING A BOLD BELIEVER

*Philip said to Him, "Lord, show us the Father,
and it is enough for us."*
—John 14:8

PHILIP

■ MEANING OF NAME
The name Philip comes from Greek *Philippos* meaning "friend of horses."

■ VOCATION
Fisherman

■ ORIGIN
Bethsaida

■ WHEN CALLED BY CHRIST
In Galilee (John 1:43)

■ GEOGRAPHY OF MINISTRY AND DEATH
"He labored diligently in Upper Asia, and suffered martyrdom at Heliopolis, in Phrygia. He was scourged, thrown into prison, and afterwards crucified, A.D. 54."[1]

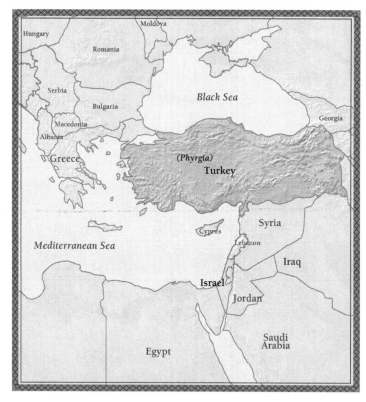

When Jesus found Philip in Galilee and said, "Follow Me" (John 1:43), Philip didn't hesitate. He immediately followed. As a probable disciple of John the Baptist, Philip had likely anticipated this day. He knew what Moses and the prophets had written. And he had probably heard John speak of the Anointed One who was coming, one whose sandals even John wasn't fit to untie. Imagine the exhilaration that must've coursed through Philip as he looked for his friend Nathanael to share the good news, "We have found Him" (1:45).

As a disciple, Philip started out great — full of anticipation, faith, and eagerness. But, although he believed in Jesus with a sincere heart, Philip struggled to fully understand who Jesus was. Following a tiring day of ministry, Jesus and the Twelve noticed a large crowd forming around them. Jesus had compassion on the hungry people who had been following Him all day, and He wanted to feed them. He also planned to teach His disciples who He really was. Jesus singled out Philip and asked, "Where can we buy bread to feed all these people?" (6:5 NLT).

The disciple's earthbound, rational mind prevented him from seeing Jesus as the solution. Despite watching Jesus perform one miracle after another, Philip's faith hit a roadblock. "Even if we worked for months, we wouldn't have enough money to feed them!" (6:7 NLT).

When faced with the challenge of finding food for the huge crowd, Philip's confidence wavered. He didn't know how to trust Jesus to provide bread for the people. He didn't realize how small the amount of money needed was to the Creator of the universe. Feeble faith stood in the way of bold trust in the Messiah.

Jesus didn't have to ask for Philip's help; the Lord knew what He planned to do before He asked. But in His grace, Jesus tested Philip in order to bring the disciple face-to-face with His power and identity. Just as God had provided heavenly bread for the Israelites in the wilderness, God had provided Jesus, the heavenly, life-giving "bread" for all who believe in Him. Jesus knew that as Philip and the other disciples started to understand who He really was and began to put their beliefs into practice, their faith would grow. And as their faith grew, Jesus could trust them with more difficult tasks, even the responsibility of making disciples and taking the gospel to the ends of the earth.

Even though Philip failed the test that day on the hillside, his trust in Messiah's powerful provision undoubtedly matured. Carrying baskets of unending loaves and fish to thousands of men, women, and children began to prepare Philip to believe Jesus's revelation of Himself as the Bread of Life and to trust Him as Provider, even when reason challenged his faith. But Philip needed more fortification.

As Jesus's last days approached, He took the Twelve to the Upper Room to prepare them for His death. He encouraged His friends, shaken by His impending crucifixion, not to let their hearts be overwhelmed but instead look forward to the day when they would live with Him in the Father's house. Jesus reminded them that He alone could give them, and anyone, access to God the Father. As the exact representation of the Father's nature (Hebrews 1:3), only Jesus could make the Father known: "I am the way, and the truth, and the life; no one comes to the Father but through Me. If you had known Me, you would have known My Father also; from now on you know Him, and have seen Him" (John 14:6–7).

But Philip still didn't get it, "Lord, show us the Father, and it is enough for us" (14:8). Jesus's patient but firm response reveals the core of Philip's deficient faith: "Have I been so long with you, and yet you have not come to know Me, Philip?" (14:9).

Philip struggled to believe that Jesus, the Man who had walked and talked with him for years, was not just a man but deity in the flesh — 100 percent God and 100 percent man (14:9–12). But Jesus understood Philip's struggle and promised to send a Helper, the Holy Spirit, who would empower not just Philip but all disciples to believe and obey Jesus's words (14:15–21).

After Philip acknowledged the incarnation and Jesus Christ's true identity, and later received the indwelling Holy Spirit at Pentecost (Acts 2:1–4), he served the church faithfully. He and the other apostles committed themselves to studying and teaching God's Word and equipping the growing church to boldly trust Jesus (6:2–4).

So what happened to Philip after his appearance in Acts 6? Several sources attest that Philip preached in northern Asia Minor (modern-day Turkey), contending for the faith and teaching about Jesus's incarnation, death, resurrection, and future return. Philip, along with the other apostles who were empowered and commissioned by Christ, continued to perform miracles that authenticated the words they spoke (Acts 4:16; 5:12–16). Philip's bold proclamation of the gospel won many to Christ, including many who had believed in the so-called "gods." Not surprisingly, the authorities in Heliopolis saw Philip as a threat to their religion and way of life. So they threw the bold disciple into prison and crucified him.[2]

We all struggle to trust God to meet our needs and work miraculously when reason tells us to doubt. But our faith grows when we find ourselves in situations where we're forced to come face-to-face with Jesus's identity as the Bread of Life. When Philip finally accepted Jesus as the Creator, the Sustainer, the eternal Son of God, and the only way to the Father, Philip became a bold believer. But his faith had to be tested before he was ready to go through fire. Like Philip, as we acknowledge our triune God as all-powerful and loving and step out in faith when reason tells us to stop, our trust will deepen, our boldness will grow, and our ministry will flourish.

—*Malia Rodriguez*

The Rest of the Story: John 14

TAKE IT TO HEART

How does acknowledging Jesus Christ's identity give you courage? When was the last time you stepped out in faith when reason told you not to? How did you grow stronger as a result?

NATHANAEL

BREAKING DOWN BARRIERS

*Nathanael answered Him, "Rabbi, You are
the Son of God; You are the King of Israel."
—John 1:49*

NATHANAEL

■ MEANING OF NAME

The Hebrew name Nathanael means "God has given."

Many commentators equate Nathanael, who only appears in John's gospel, with Bartholomew, who is paired with Philip in the Synoptic Gospels. Bartholomew, who does not show up in John's gospel, likely had another name since the surname Bartholomew means "son of Tolmai."[1]

■ VOCATION

Fisherman (John 21:1–3)

■ ORIGIN

Cana (21:2)

■ WHEN CALLED BY CHRIST

When Jesus called the Twelve

■ GEOGRAPHY OF MINISTRY AND DEATH

"Preached in several countries, and having translated the Gospel of Matthew into the language of India, he propagated it in that country. He was at length cruelly beaten and then crucified by the impatient idolaters."[2]

Perhaps as he sat in the shade escaping the beating sun, Nathanael's mind focused on heavenly things. As a "genuine son of Israel" (John 1:47 NLT), Nathanael might have regularly confessed his sins, prayed for wisdom, and asked for God's help to keep a pure heart. Nathanael also would have known the history of his people—God's people—who frequently forgot Yahweh and yielded to idolatry. They were double-minded, but Nathanael took seriously God's command to be holy as He is holy (Leviticus 11:44–45). As a model Israelite, Nathanael would have strived to live a life without guile, free of deception. He would've sought God's favor in everything and spent time meditating on God's Word, perhaps under that very fig tree.

But one corner of Nathanael's mind seems to have remained untouched by God's Spirit. Nathanael had apparently become prideful, looking down on others who didn't live exemplary lives. He, along with most Jews, looked forward to Messiah's arrival. But when Philip found Nathanael under that fig tree and told him they'd found the One Moses wrote about, Nathanael couldn't believe it. The Man Philip had found claimed His home to be the town of Nazareth (John 1:45–46). Nathanael hoped for a righteous Messiah who would break the bonds of the unholy Romans and rule Israel with justice. And of all towns, a just and holy ruler surely couldn't come from Nazareth.

"'Nazareth!' exclaimed Nathanael. 'Can anything good come from Nazareth?'" (1:46 NLT).

By asking if anything *good* could come from Nazareth, Nathanael likely revealed his perception of the city as immoral. Many people may have looked down on the small town in southern Galilee because of its lax ethics and religious carelessness.[3] Furthermore, the Old Testament descriptions of Messiah just didn't seem to fit with Nazareth. Nathanael would've been looking for someone who matched his interpretation of Isaiah's prophecy. The Servant of the Lord would rule with compassion and bring justice to the whole earth (Isaiah 42). The Servant would represent God, the Holy One of Israel, and restore His people to Him (49:1–7). Nathanael waited for *this* majestic Messiah, not some humble man from Nazareth.

So when Philip told Nathanael to come meet the Messiah—the One foretold in the Law and the Prophets, a *Nazarene*—Nathanael rolled his eyes. "'Come and see for yourself,' Philip replied" (John 1:46 NLT).

As Nathanael and Philip approached, Jesus, knowing Nathanael's pre-conceptions, extended grace. Jesus praised Nathanael's pure heart and his desire to please God, calling him "a genuine son of Israel—a man of complete integrity" (John 1:47 NLT). Then Jesus proved His omniscience by revealing Nathanael's whereabouts before their meeting—completely alone under the fig tree. Nathanael responded by confessing Jesus as "the Son of God . . . the King of Israel" (1:49).

In response to Nathanael's confession, Jesus promised to show the future apostle even more amazing, supernatural things. Imagine how Nathanael, who had longed to see the Messiah's reign, felt as Jesus told him and the others: "You will all see heaven open and the angels of God going up and down on the Son of Man, the one who is the stairway between heaven and earth" (1:51 NLT). As a result of Nathanael's faith, Jesus promised to open his eyes to the Messiah, the Son of God and Son of Man, as He provided a way for sinful human beings to connect with the holy God.

In Genesis 28, as Jacob slept after fleeing his brother whose birthright he had stolen, he dreamt of a stairway connecting heaven and earth with God standing sovereign above it. The angels traveling up and down symbolized God's care for and activity in the affairs of His people—sending His angels to achieve His plans on earth. Such a stairway wouldn't have been a new concept to those who heard about Jacob's dream. Jacob's dream foreshadowed God's provision of Jesus Christ—the God-Man who connects heaven to earth—and reminded the Israelites of God's faithful character.

Nathanael would've recognized Jesus's reference to Jacob's dream at Bethel. Nathanael also would've understood that by claiming to be the stairway to heaven, Jesus had revealed Himself as the Messiah—the bridge between sinful people and holy God. And, as a good Israelite, Nathanael would have wanted more than anything to honor God and see His holiness fill the earth. Though we don't know much about this disciple's life after his first encounter with the Savior, we do know Nathanael responded to Jesus with faith and became one of the twelve chosen by Christ to be in His inner circle.

Nathanael's story prompts us to examine our hearts for presumption—the same barrier that stood in his way when Jesus called him. Nathanael presumed God would carry out His plan to redeem His people and give them an everlasting ruler in a way that made sense to Nathanael. But God often surprises us. Thankfully, when Jesus revealed His power and identity, Nathanael abandoned his preconceived ideas and bowed before his Lord. Presumption gave way to confession.

When God brings people into our lives who don't meet our standards or when He presents us with opportunities outside our comfort zones, how do we react? Prideful presumption prevents us from seeing God's plan and joining Him where He is at work. Like Nathanael, we must allow God to blast through our walls of presumption and lead us to confess our trust in Him.

—*Malia Rodriguez*

The Rest of the Story: Luke 15:11–32; John 1:47–51

TAKE IT TO HEART

How has your confession of Jesus as God's Son changed the way you interact with others? Has pride or presumption ever kept you from participating in God's work?

JAMES
WASTED FOR GLORY

Going on from there He saw two other brothers,
James the son of Zebedee, and John his brother, in
the boat with Zebedee their father, mending their nets;
and He called them. — Matthew 4:21

JAMES

■ **MEANING OF NAME**
James is the Greek version of Jacob in Hebrew, which means "supplanter."

■ **VOCATION**
Fisherman, along with his brother, John; partners with Peter and Andrew

■ **ORIGIN**
Galilee

■ **WHEN CALLED BY CHRIST**
Early in Jesus's ministry

■ **DEATH**
The first apostle martyred, beheaded by Herod Agrippa I

■ **GEOGRAPHY OF MINISTRY**
Galilee and Judea

J esus stood in the center of several concentric circles—groups of individuals who numbered from multiple thousands to only a few. The Lord related to the masses, but within that largest circle, Jesus had a smaller circle of true followers. From that group, He selected twelve disciples whom He designated apostles, men who were to be with Him everywhere He went. From that tight-knit group, Jesus handpicked an unofficial three who would see what no one else saw (Matthew 17:1–2; Mark 5:37–43). Simon Peter, James, and John—the only apostles who received new names—formed this tightest circle.

As brothers, James and John shared one nickname: "Sons of Thunder." In fact, the Gospels never mention James without John; the brothers were inseparable. The day Jesus approached them by the Sea of Galilee appears in Scripture as the first time the Master spoke to them, but they possibly had known each other all their lives. If the brothers' mother, Salome, was the sister of Jesus's mother, Mary, as is commonly thought, then these inseparable siblings were cousins of the Savior (compare Matthew 27:56; Mark 16:1; John 19:25). When Jesus called to James and John from the shore, they *immediately* left their boat—and their father—and followed Him (Matthew 4:21–22). If they were all cousins, the brothers' quick response seems less impulsive. However, pure familial devotion might not have been the only motive for their sudden departure.

The name James actually renders "Jacob" in the Greek New Testament. (We have the King *James* Version to thank for the misnomer.) The Hebrew name Jacob means "one who supplants." Although James's parents likely only intended to name their son after the great patriarch, what happened on Jesus's final journey to Jerusalem links James to Jacob's character as well.

On Jesus's last pilgrimage to Jerusalem, many traveled with Him and His disciples—including the mother of James and John. The brothers approached the Master in private to ask a favor. (In truth, James and John got their mommy to ask Jesus for them.) "Command that in Your kingdom these two sons of mine may sit one on Your right and one on Your left" (20:21). The fact that James and John got their mother to make their special request of Jesus gives weight to the likelihood that the brothers were Jesus's cousins. What's more, if they were kin, their families would have walked those same roads dozens of times as they made their way up to Jerusalem for the annual feasts (Luke 2:44).

In other words, James and John most likely pulled the family card, asked for the best seats in the kingdom, and used Jesus's aunt to try to make it happen. Maybe their hope for a little sanctified nepotism had motivated them to leave their father's boat in such a hurry three years earlier. For sure, their request on that last pilgrimage revealed what their motive had become. They wanted glory, and Jesus was the ticket.

Jesus directed His answer to Salome's question toward James and his younger brother: "You do not know what you are asking. Are you able to drink the cup that I am about to drink?" The "cup" represented Jesus's impending execution in Jerusalem. The brothers blathered, "We are able" (Matthew 20:22). Then Jesus added, "My cup you shall drink" (20:23).

After a week in Jerusalem and a final Passover meal together, Jesus asked the three in His inner circle to join Him in Gethsemane. The Master confided that He wanted them to pray with Him, for He suffered grief over what lay ahead. But instead of supporting Jesus, James and his pals fell asleep . . . that is, until Jesus woke them and the rattling of swords and the light of torches exposed the soldiers who had come to arrest Jesus.

In a fit of fear, James and every other disciple abandoned the Lord and fled like rabbits. Perhaps Jesus's question echoed in James's ears as he zigzagged through the olive trees in the black of night.

Are you able to drink the cup that I am about to drink?

The absolute disillusionment that followed Jesus's crucifixion raked the pride and selfish ambition from James and all the Lord's glory-bound disciples. But then mourning gave way to joy as Jesus rose from the dead and ascended to heaven, having commissioned His church to make disciples.

For eleven years the young church struggled and grew until King Herod Agrippa arrested some of Jesus's followers in Jerusalem, including James, whom Agrippa ordered executed by sword (Acts 12:2). The suddenness and brevity of the account leaves us stunned. And it begs a question: Why would Jesus choose James to join His innermost circle only to allow the disciple's execution so soon after the birth of the church? All that time, all that training — gone. Certainly someone else was more expendable? From our perspective, it seems a waste.

The shortness of James's life would have had a jolting influence on the ministry of his brother John—the apostle who lived the longest and became the apostle of love. James was the first apostle to suffer martyrdom; John was the last. An early death by the sword—not quite the glory James requested of Jesus that day along the road. It was, in fact, much more.

As the executioner approached James's prison cell, the disciple's conversation with Jesus must have rung in his ears. *Are you able to drink the cup I am about to drink?* The guards bared James's neck, and he heard the *shing* of the sword jerked from its scabbard. *We are able.* The soldier raised his sword above James's head. *My cup you shall drink.* And then, in a moment, James's conversation with Jesus was no longer just a memory but a reality—as he beheld the risen Christ again face-to-face. The first apostle home. The first to experience glory—far beyond what he requested.

—Wayne Stiles

The Rest of the Story: Matthew 20:17–28

TAKE IT TO HEART

What motivates you to follow Jesus? Are you willing to surrender your life? If so, are you willing to do that daily—even if you live to an old age?

MATTHEW

REDEEMED TO HEAL

And Levi gave a big reception for Him in his house; and there was a great crowd of tax collectors and other people who were reclining at the table with them. —Luke 5:29

MATTHEW

■ MEANING OF NAME
Matthew derives from an Aramaic word meaning, "gift of Yahweh," while Levi was a Hebrew name meaning "joined to."

■ VOCATION
Tax collector

■ ORIGIN
Possibly Capernaum, where he worked near a major highway collecting tolls for the Roman government

■ WHEN CALLED BY CHRIST
Early in Jesus's ministry, just after the Lord healed a paralytic

■ DEATH
Run through with a spear in Egypt

■ GEOGRAPHY OF MINISTRY
Ethiopia and Egypt

I n the ancient world, weary travelers loved nothing more than the sight of the next town along the highway. Such oases offered the promise of refreshment, the opportunity to rest tired feet, and the facilities to water and feed their entire traveling parties—animals included. Travelers found relief in these places, the kind of temporary healing that steels one for the journey yet unfinished.

However, every so often near one of those towns along the highway, fatigued travelers encountered someone else: a man, flanked by intimidating soldiers, with his hand out in the name of Rome, the foreign government that ruled the land. The Roman government required funds to build and maintain their empire-wide road system. Furthermore, the Romans needed money to maintain their domination in the region. With the wealth they collected, they fed soldiers, supported local arms of Roman government, and built magnificent structures in honor of the emperors. To amass such monetary resources, the Romans employed local citizens as tax collectors. In a high-traffic region like the Promised Land, one of the most effective means of collection involved stationing these men in booths along major highways. Then, as travelers passed, they had to stop and pay the required amount.

In Israel, tax collectors were subject to the hatred and disdain of their communities. Many Jews believed that these men had compromised themselves by working for the oppressive enemy. And many tax collectors, in fact, had compromised their integrity in another way. Out on their own with little regulation, most tax collectors reinforced their negative reputation by taking more in taxes than the government actually required and using the extra to fund their own lavish lifestyles.

When Jesus called Matthew (called "Levi," according to Mark and Luke) to be one of His disciples, the Lord couldn't have chosen anyone more isolated from "polite," religious society. No one among the self-proclaimed righteous would have been caught dead with someone like Matthew.

For tax collectors, the luxuries of the day were just one extorted tax-payer away. Unlike others who struggled and scraped just to get by, Matthew never lacked for a firm roof over his head, expensive clothes on his back, or bountiful feasts at his table. And yet, at the call of Jesus, the tax collector immediately left his booth unmanned (Luke 5:27–28).

Matthew abandoned his comfortable life to follow One who had no place to lay His head, whose clothes were simple, and who relied on the kindness of women and children in order to eat. No longer would Matthew inflict pain and suffering on the poor by overtaxing them as they sought to get from one town to the next. The apostle followed a new master who had a profoundly different vision for how to treat people in this world.

To illustrate his remarkable change of heart, Matthew took Jesus to his comfortable home and staged a banquet with the Lord as the guest of honor. The disciple sent word to all his friends, and as he had no friends among "polite" company, the house quickly filled with sinners and outcasts from religious society (Mark 2:15; Luke 5:29).

Such a gathering attracted a great deal of attention in the community. Religious leaders grumbled that a good man like Jesus would spend time with the lowlifes gathered in Matthew's home. Eventually, they complained to Jesus's disciples about the Lord, thinking that Jesus couldn't hear (Luke 5:30). However, Jesus heard their complaints and revealed His own comfort with the company He kept: "It is not those who are well who need a physician, but those who are sick. I have not come to call the righteous but sinners to repentance" (5:31–32).

Not only did Jesus not apologize for His behavior, He actually affirmed that sinners like the ones beside Him at Matthew's table were just the kind of people He needed to surround Himself with! The significance of this declaration would not have been lost on Matthew. The new disciple had spent who knows how many years of his adult life as the butt of derisive jokes and as the object of withering scorn from religious leaders. Now, he had found someone who recognized that it isn't through angry pronouncements of judgment and fear that people like Matthew turn their lives around. It's through the work the Spirit does when a person responds to the offer to follow Jesus. By dropping his thievery and following Jesus, Matthew pursued a different path, one that brought healing instead of hurt (Mark 6:7–13).

Matthew illustrates the radical change that takes place when we decide to truly follow Jesus. No longer do we choose the option of dabbling in evil and taking advantage of others for our own gain. Instead, we have the responsibility of pursuing good and bringing healing and help to others wherever we go. Jesus redeemed Matthew from a life of inflicting pain on others, freeing him to give liberally in whatever ways he could. The Lord does the same for us. This kind of freedom is a gift any way we look at it, but it's a gift that comes with a high personal cost, for it requires that we give away rather than take for ourselves. But as we give, we gain the eternal rewards of joy, peace, and contentment found in the knowledge that we are bringing good to the world. Such rewards more than outweigh the pain and difficulty we may encounter as we sacrifice to follow Jesus.

Therefore, as we meet weary travelers along the road of life, may we do all we can to ensure that they not see us as "tax collectors" looking to take advantage, but as innkeepers looking to provide rest and relief from the hard journey.

—John Adair

The Rest of the Story: Matthew 9:9–13; Mark 2:14–17; Luke 5:27–32

TAKE IT TO HEART

What does Jesus's eating comfortably with tax collectors and sinners teach you? In what concrete ways can you bring healing to the lives of people you encounter every day?

JAMES
THE SON OF ALPHAEUS
IN NINTH PLACE

They came to Jesus and woke Him up,
saying, "Master, Master, we are perishing!"
—Luke 8:24

JAMES

THE SON OF ALPHAEUS

■ **MEANING OF NAME**
James is the Greek version of Jacob in Hebrew, which means "supplanter."

■ **VOCATION**
Unknown

■ **ORIGIN**
Unknown

■ **WHEN CALLED BY CHRIST**
When Jesus gathered the Twelve

■ **DEATH**
"At the age of ninety-four he was beat [*sic*] and stoned by the Jews; and finally had his brains dashed out with a fuller's club." [1]

■ **GEOGRAPHY OF MINISTRY**
Israel

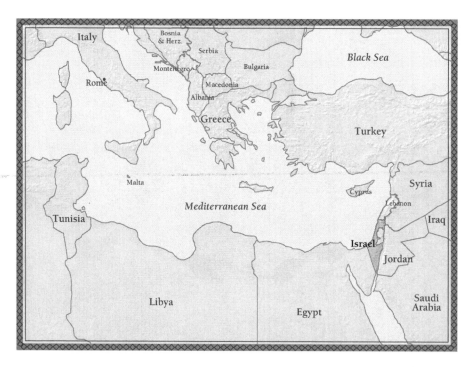

I magine being known as the little guy, as "less" than the others. That's how the Bible identifies James the son of Alphaeus. The gospel writers didn't want to confuse this James with the more prominent son of Zebedee, who along with John and Peter comprised Jesus's innermost circle. But James the son of Alphaeus still had an important role to play as one of the Messiah's select servants. Jesus had handpicked James for ministry, and like the other disciples, he left *everything* to follow the Savior (Luke 18:28).

But before James could be sent off to make disciples, Jesus had to deal with a barrier in James's spiritual life, a barrier most followers of Christ must face — fear.

James the son of Alphaeus always shows up ninth in the list of Jesus's twelve closest companions (Matthew 10:2 – 4; Mark 3:16 – 19; Luke 6:13 – 16; Acts 1:13). Though this little-known disciple lived much of his life out of the spotlight, he most likely was present any time the apostles are mentioned as a group. One such occasion revealed both James's fear and his growing faith.

Life as one of Jesus's twelve disciples never slowed down. From one village to the next, one miracle to another, these twelve men followed Jesus wherever He went. One day, a large crowd started to gather from the many towns where they had trekked. Exhausted from walking all day, James likely just wanted to rest. But Jesus took the opportunity to teach the crowd about true discipleship using two parables — one featuring a farmer scattering his seed and another featuring a lamp. Jesus explained that God's Word can only take root in soft, obedient hearts, and that once the Word has taken root, true disciples should share it openly with others (Luke 8:4 – 18). James, along with the other disciples, listened to Jesus's words. Though they didn't understand His teaching completely, they took His parables to heart. Scripture shows that the disciples wanted to follow Jesus with obedience, but often, like many of us, anxiety kept creeping into their minds (8:24).

After Jesus finished teaching the crowds, He and His disciples climbed into a boat and began to cross the Sea of Galilee. Finally, James and his friends could rest . . . until the winds and waves nearly capsized their boat. Paralyzed with fear, James and the other disciples called out to Jesus, "Master, Master, we're going to drown!" (8:24 NLT). Despite walking with Him daily, they didn't recognize the creator of the sea sitting in the boat with them. But when

Jesus calmed the storm with only a word, awe overwhelmed them. Faith began to replace fear as James and the others started to understand who Jesus really is—the God-Man who exercises complete control over every created thing. This lesson prepared James for the immediate ministry that lay on the other side of the sea, as well as for the good works God had prepared for James to do throughout his life.

This faith-fortifying event on the stormy sea punctuates a flurry of ministry activity in James's life. Through this storm, sandwiched between Jesus's powerful parables and His healing miracles, Jesus gave James an opportunity to trust Him. The Gospels only mention little James the son of Alphaeus a few times, and Acts only once, placing the disciple in the Upper Room engaged in prayer after Jesus's resurrection (Acts 1:13). Though we know very little about James, Jesus knew him inside and out. And Jesus knew exactly what it would take to train James for each step in his journey of faith.

What happened to James the son of Alphaeus after this final appearance in the Bible? How did he carry out Jesus's commission to make disciples of all nations?

We know that the resurrection of Jesus changed all the apostles' lives dramatically and that the Holy Spirit empowered them to follow Christ's call to announce God's kingdom throughout the world (1:8). Church tradition has passed down James's story, which portrays him as a man who followed the command of Jesus to serve not just for a few years but faithfully for the rest of his life. According to tradition, James taught in the Jewish synagogues telling people about Jesus and His resurrection from the dead and fearlessly revealing His identity as the very Son of God. After many years of faithful service, the Jews recognized this bold apostle as a threat to the Jewish way of life. So they stoned James the son of Alphaeus to death.[2]

Though fear plagued James in the early years of his journey with Christ, courage characterized the rest of his faithful life. James's confidence in Christ empowered him to live out his calling whether or not others acknowledged him. He accepted his place out of the limelight because he lived to make Jesus famous.

James's life prompts us to ask: *Do I have the courage to serve God boldly, even if no one ever acknowledges my hard work? Am I content to be the little one?*

Too often, the fear of obscurity keeps us from performing the tasks God gives us. We want others to acknowledge our sacrifice, so we look for ways to blow our own spiritual trumpets. But James the son of Alphaeus reminds us that serving as Christ's disciple doesn't require fame, rank, or acclaim. God loves to use faithful unknowns.

We have only to accept the positions God gives us and follow His commands as James did in his ninth position among the Twelve. And we must learn, like James, to look to Jesus for the courage to do so, even as the winds and waves whip against our lives. Whether God calms the storms or strengthens us through them, we can trust He will equip us to fulfill our calling. All He asks is that we trust Him and abandon fear.

—Malia Rodriguez

The Rest of the Story: Luke 8

TAKE IT TO HEART

What do you think it will take to prepare you for faithful ministry? What fears keep you from serving the Lord with courage? Are you content with obscurity, or are you afraid of living outside the limelight?

THADDAEUS

FINDING GOD IN OBEDIENCE

Judas (not Iscariot) said to Him, "Lord, what then has happened that You are going to disclose Yourself to us and not to the world?"
—John 14:22

THADDAEUS

■ MEANING OF NAME
Judas is the Greek version of the Hebrew, Judah, which means "God is praised," while Thaddaeus is possibly a nickname related to large-heartedness or courage.

■ VOCATION
Unknown

■ ORIGIN
Unknown

■ WHEN CALLED BY CHRIST
Early in Jesus's ministry, when the Lord assembled the Twelve

■ DEATH
Beaten to death in Berytus (Beirut, Lebanon)

■ GEOGRAPHY OF MINISTRY
Throughout much of the Middle East, from Judea and Samaria to Syria and Edessa

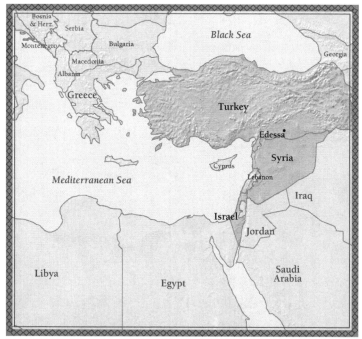

*F*ollow Me.

Those words, spoken by Jesus to a number of His apostles, carry a great deal of meaning. On the surface, they're simple. Jesus wanted these men to literally follow Him as He journeyed throughout Israel and other nearby areas. And they did, traveling with Jesus as a group of learners, watching Him minister and listening to Him teach. However, when Jesus called these men to follow, He had in mind much more than the direction of their feet.

Jesus expected these "following" apostles not just to listen and watch but to *do* as well. He provided opportunities for them to go out themselves, teaching and ministering—*following* Jesus with their words and deeds (Matthew 10:5–8). All of this was preparation for a time to come when Jesus would no longer be physically present with them, a time when this ragged group of simple men would be tasked with taking the blessed message of God's kingdom into the world, far from the humble hamlets of their origins.

Among Jesus's followers was a man called Thaddaeus (Matthew 10:3; Mark 3:18). Luke and John called this same man Judas (Luke 6:16; John 14:22; Acts 1:13). While Scripture offers no reason for the different names, no one would blink an eye if a man named Judas among Jesus's followers decided to change his name after Judas Iscariot betrayed the Lord. Avoiding presumed guilt and harsh looks might have been reason enough for this apostle to start going by Thaddaeus. Furthermore, as Thaddaeus means "large-hearted," in the sense of someone being courageous, the disciples could have given this "good Judas" the nickname Thaddaeus in recognition of one of his better qualities.

Whatever the reason, Thaddaeus—or Judas—was named in the Bible for the first time when Jesus called together the large group of disciples that had been following Him and chose twelve from that number to serve as His inner circle. Thaddaeus found himself named among those appointed by Christ to be with Him and to preach and cast out demons in His name (Mark 3:14–19). Before becoming one of the group known simply as "the Twelve," Thaddaeus had likely been following Jesus for some time as part of the larger crowd. That Jesus singled out Thaddaeus as a part of this smaller, intimate group illustrated that Jesus had a special purpose for the man.

Yet, throughout the Gospels, Thaddaeus remains silent. He doesn't stand out from the Twelve until Jesus's lengthy conversation with the apostles after the Last Supper (John 14–17), and then only briefly. As Jesus spoke with the remaining faithful eleven on the eve of offering His own life as a sacrifice for all humanity, Thaddaeus spoke up. Named by John as "Judas (not Iscariot)," Thaddaeus asked Jesus a question: "Lord, what then has happened that You are going to disclose Yourself to us and not to the world?" (14:22).

Jesus had been speaking about the Holy Spirit who would come to help the Lord's disciples practice obedience. God's followers have always had difficulty translating their love for Him into obedience, and while Jesus understood this difficulty, He did not lower the standard: love yields obedience (14:15). In His wisdom, the Lord knew our weakness. He knew we would need strength from the Holy Spirit if we ever hoped to follow God's Son well. And if, through the empowering of the Holy Spirit, we would love and obey Him, Jesus promised to disclose Himself to us (14:21).

But why the limitation? Why would Jesus reveal Himself only to the obedient instead of to the whole world? To answer Thaddaeus's question, Jesus reaffirmed His original statement—He makes His abode with those who love Him and who, therefore, keep His words. Those who do not love and obey the Lord will not find Christ abiding with them (14:23–24).

While Jesus's words may have sounded strikingly different than anything the apostles had heard before, God has always dealt with His people in a similar fashion. In the Old Testament era, God valued obedience in His people from beginning to end. The garden of Eden witnessed perfect fellowship between God and humanity while Adam and Eve remained obedient. But the couple's disobedience broke that relationship, leaving them expelled from the garden and distant from God (Genesis 3:8–13, 24). The connection between obedience and God's presence was later codified in the Mosaic Law—He would make His dwelling with those who kept His commandments (Leviticus 26:3, 11–12). After hundreds of years in the Promised Land, God's people were exiled and God's glory departed, all because they chose disobedience over and over again (Ezekiel 10:18).

Jesus's teaching to the apostles was, therefore, right in line with what the Old Testament had revealed about God's relationship to His people. The major difference came after Jesus died, was resurrected, and ascended. The Lord sent the Holy Spirit to help His people remain obedient. Thaddaeus's question gave Jesus the opportunity to underscore a significant truth for the apostles then and for Christians today: when people of faith follow after Jesus in obedience, He increasingly makes Himself known.

Thaddaeus, a little-known disciple, raised an issue vital for all those who seek to follow Christ. When we obey God, we know Him better than we do when we disregard His words and live according to our own ideals. Attentiveness breeds knowledge. We follow, and He abides.

If we follow Jesus by attempting to align our actions with our words, we will see obedience flourish from our faith commitments. And as we struggle forward, we do so with a remarkable promised reward: greater knowledge of our God. The better attention we pay to His words—not just remembering them but obeying them—the more we can affirm that, yes, this God who has allowed us to find Him knows us . . . and we know Him.

—John Adair

The Rest of the Story: John 14–17

TAKE IT TO HEART

Does it surprise you that obedience and knowing God are so closely connected? In what ways has obedience brought you into a greater knowledge of God?

SIMON
THE ZEALOT
ZEALOUS FOR THE LORD

"But all this has taken place to fulfill the Scriptures of the prophets." Then all the disciples left Him and fled. —Matthew 26:56

SIMON
THE ZEALOT

■ **MEANING OF NAME**
In Hebrew, Simon means "he who hears." *Zealot* refers to a political and religious group around the time of Jesus that was willing to take military action to overthrow Rome.

■ **VOCATION**
Disciple of Jesus

■ **ORIGIN**
Cana (Mark 3:18)

■ **WHEN CALLED BY CHRIST**
When Jesus gathered the Twelve

■ **GEOGRAPHY OF MINISTRY AND DEATH**
Simon the Zealot "preached the Gospel in Mauritania, Africa, and even in Britain, in which latter country he was crucified, A.D. 74." [1]

Scripture tells us little about the man listed as "Simon the Zealot" among the twelve disciples. But, although we don't know much about Simon, we do know that he may have politically and religiously tied himself to the Zealots before Jesus found him.[2] The Zealots were a fanatical, sometimes militant, Jewish nationalist group who hated Roman rule and devoted themselves to Jewish law.

As a Zealot, Simon would not have wanted to pay taxes to Rome and would have mocked civil servants and even considered them traitors. So everyone must have expected sparks to fly when Jesus called both Simon the Zealot and Matthew the tax collector, not only to join Him in ministry but to serve *together* as His apostles. The situation illustrated the truth that Jesus's call reaches people of all walks of life and His kingdom encompasses them all. Since Scripture records no "sparks," we can conclude that Simon and Matthew learned this lesson well and came to love each other and work side by side in ministry. Their zeal for their Lord united them.

Zeal can be good when it's directed toward the right object. When the Jews transformed the temple — God's house — from the central place of worship to a place of business, Jesus's anger caused Him to knock over tables and chase out vendors with a whip (John 2:15–17). As the disciples witnessed Jesus's zeal on display, they remembered King David's words in Psalm 69:9, "For zeal for Your house has consumed me, and the reproaches of those who reproach You have fallen on me." David, the rejected but anointed king of Israel, faced reproach because he worshiped the Lord and honored Him each day. Though at times David felt like God had abandoned him, the king knew God would ultimately call his enemies to account and bless him for his devotion.

David's zeal for the Lord fueled his faithfulness, and his words in Psalm 69 mirror Jesus Christ's life. The rejected Messiah faced persecution, hatred, and suspicion every day of His ministry. And at His crucifixion, Jesus even felt forsaken by His Father. But throughout His life, a passionate commitment to God's glory and God's will directed Jesus's thoughts, words, and actions. His zeal for God kept Him going when the pressure seemed too intense.

Appropriate zeal is passion under control. Though Jesus overturned tables in His anger, He never lost His cool. Jesus didn't fly off the handle.

Before meeting the Messiah, Simon, like most Zealots, probably flew off the handle any time anyone threatened the political or religious supremacy of the Jews. But after walking with Jesus and listening to Him, Simon began to learn how to channel his zeal and direct it toward a worthy purpose—defending God's glory and His character.

But after nearly three years of following Christ and learning to direct his passion toward God's glory, Simon discovered his zeal wasn't yet pure enough to get him through the most trying time of his spiritual life.

After sharing a final meal with His closest disciples, Jesus took them to Gethsemane. He told Simon the Zealot and His other disciples to wait while He went away to pray (Matthew 26:36). But as Jesus poured out His anguish to the Father, Simon and the others fell asleep. Finally, the arrival of Judas and a band of soldiers interrupted their nap (26:44–46). The disciples trembled with fear in the midst of the angry men armed with heavy clubs and sharp swords . . . and they fled (26:56). They left Jesus in the hands of the enemy.

Zealous, passionate Simon, along with every other disciple, deserted Jesus during His trial and crucifixion.

Although Simon the Zealot doesn't appear in the Gospels and Acts more than a few times, church tradition tells us that he led a life of fruitful ministry. After Jesus's resurrection and ascension, Simon carried out the Great Commission with passion and courage. Instead of following the Zealots—and blazing his own political and religious trail while touting the glory of Israel—Simon followed Jesus's command to serve others humbly and to make disciples. The apostle became zealous for God's glory. According to *Fox's Book of Martyrs*, Simon preached the gospel in Mauritania, Africa. Afterward, he traveled to Britain, where he was supposedly crucified in AD 74. For more than forty years after Jesus's death and resurrection, Simon zealously proclaimed the gospel.

Zeal should lead us to live lives of daily sacrifice, to defend the Lord and His character, and to give up our own comfort and desires when God calls us to. But, like the Zealots of Jesus's day, too often we direct our energy toward what will bring *us* glory. We must ask ourselves: *What do I spend the most time doing? What evokes the most passion from me?* If our answers to these questions don't involve honoring God and obeying Him, then we may have the wrong kind of zeal.

If we want to learn, like Simon did, what genuine, godly zeal looks like, all we have to do is look at Jesus—the very Son of God who set aside His divine rights and instead suffered and died for sinners (Philippians 2:6–8). With God's glory at the forefront of His mind, Jesus lived with the singular desire to obey His heavenly Father. Jesus transformed Simon's life, teaching him to have the same kind of zeal for God's glory—the kind that moved the disciple to passionately obey His Lord and to be unified with others who put Him first. Our Lord can do the same for us.

—*Malia Rodriguez*

The Rest of the Story: Psalm 69; Matthew 26:36–56

TAKE IT TO HEART

Do you look for opportunities to use your natural passions for God's glory? Do others know you more by what you are for than what you are against?

_____

_____

_____

_____

_____

_____

_____

_____

_____

_____

THOMAS
RESURRECTED FROM DOUBT

Thomas answered and said to Him,
"My Lord and my God!"
—John 20:28

THOMAS

■ MEANING OF NAME
The Aramaic name Thomas, along with the Greek name, Didymus, means "twin."

■ VOCATION
Possibly worked as a carpenter

■ ORIGIN
Unknown

■ WHEN CALLED BY CHRIST
Early in Jesus's ministry, when the Lord assembled the Twelve

■ DEATH
Poisoned by a dart in India

■ GEOGRAPHY OF MINISTRY
Thomas ministered to the east of Israel, traveling as far as Persia (modern-day Iran) and even into India.

Impending death pushed the messenger beyond the banks of the Jordan into the region of Perea. John the Baptizer had ministered in that place, calling people to believe in the coming Messiah. Now the Messiah Himself had come, sitting with the Twelve outside the Promised Land to avoid the dangers that lurked within. The messenger sought out Jesus to deliver devastating news: *Death had come near to Lazarus of Bethany. Would Jesus come and send off this wicked intruder?*

Instead of rushing to His sick friend's side, Jesus simply assured His apostles that death would not get the final word (John 11:4). They were likely relieved at this decision. The last time they ventured into Judea, angry Jews threatened Jesus's life (10:39). But Jesus never acted out of fear. He had no intention of avoiding Judea altogether. The Lord waited two days, announced that Lazarus had died, and called the apostles to go with Him to Bethany (11:6, 14–15).

Thomas then spoke up, declaring to the rest of the Twelve, "Let us also go, so that we may die with Him" (11:16). At first, Thomas's courage flies off the page. While the others hesitated, this apostle immediately announced his willingness to give his life to follow Jesus. Thomas believed so deeply in the Man and His mission — or at least what Thomas thought was the mission — that he declared his desire to follow Jesus into any danger.

But Thomas's words not only displayed courage; they also revealed his comfort with the idea of dying with Jesus *right then*. The apostle's declaration illustrated a lack of understanding of the Father's ultimate plan. In Thomas's mind, the disciples had had a nice run. They had done some good. If it was time for this small group of twelve to get wiped off the map, so be it. In other words, for Thomas, death in Bethany was a legitimate end to Jesus's story . . . even as Jesus went to resurrect His friend from the dead!

Thomas understood only the logical conclusion right in front of him. He failed to consider God's mysterious ways, though unfathomable power and wisdom characterized Jesus's entire ministry. The Lord's deeds with Lazarus in Bethany would foreshadow His own death and resurrection, but Jesus knew His time had not yet come.

Thomas reappears in John 14, this time after the Last Supper. As Jesus taught the eleven — Judas Iscariot had already left the Upper Room to continue his work of betrayal—He talked about going to prepare a place for His followers. The Lord told the men that they knew the way to this place (John 14:2–4). Thomas voiced the group's confusion: "Lord, we do not know where You are going, how do we know the way?" (14:5). Thomas didn't even know what place Jesus was talking about, much less the way to get there!

Again, Thomas's life places the mystery of our ultimate destination before us. The apostle thought death the only option as the group headed back to Bethany. And after he and the others survived that trip, he still had little idea where they were headed, even as Jesus made clear the way to get to that mysterious destination in the Father's presence: "I am the way, and the truth, and the life; no one comes to the Father but through Me" (14:6). The way forward for Jesus's followers remained shrouded in the haze of God's infinite wisdom.

Thomas's final, unique appearance in the gospel narratives offers a fitting end to his journey through the Gospels. Jesus appeared to the apostles on the same day of His resurrection. Most of them had regathered after scattering in the aftermath of Jesus's trial and crucifixion, but Thomas was still not present. The apostles' joy at seeing the resurrected Lord was unmistakable as they later relayed their experience to Thomas. But because of pain, fear, or something else, Thomas refused to believe . . . unless he saw this resurrected Jesus in the flesh (20:24–25). Jesus's death had shaken this faithful apostle. His imagination did not extend to resurrection—despite the testimony of his closest friends.

Doubts remained with Thomas eight days. His famous nickname—Doubting Thomas—is somewhat unfair in this light. He only doubted eight days! In Thomas's other appearances in Scripture, he commits to follow Jesus even to death. To the end, Thomas clearly wanted to know where Jesus was going so he could follow. His devotion was pure, his courage never faltered, but logic limited his faith.

In the midst of Thomas's struggle, the disciples gathered together again. This time, Thomas joined them. And when Jesus appeared in the closed room, the reality of resurrected flesh overwhelmed the apostle. Thomas dropped to his knees and testified, "My Lord and my God!" (20:28).

Notice that Jesus never told Thomas where exactly they were going. Thomas never received ultimate clarity on the location of this "Father's house." However, first to Thomas, and now to us through the life of this apostle recorded in Scripture, Jesus revealed that while the next steps in our journeys may be unclear, we can never go wrong by following Him. Jesus has conquered death, and with it, sin and sorrow and pain. He is the way to meet the Father—even as heaven's location remains a mystery to our limited minds. As we confess Him as Lord and God *without* seeing Him (John 20:29), we will receive the blessing of following wherever He leads, with faith—not sight—as our guide.

—*John Adair*

The Rest of the Story: John 11:1–16; 14:1–6; 20:24–28

TAKE IT TO HEART

How do Thomas's doubts about the resurrection inform your faith in Jesus? What does Jesus's ambiguity about the disciples' ultimate destination teach you about the nature of faith?

JUDAS

ISCARIOT
OPPRESSED BY REGRET

When Judas, who had betrayed Him, saw that
He had been condemned, he felt remorse.
—Matthew 27:3

JUDAS ISCARIOT

■ MEANING OF NAME
Judas is the Greek version of the Hebrew, Judah, which means "God is praised." Iscariot most likely means "man from Kerioth."

■ VOCATION
Unknown

■ ORIGIN
Kerioth

■ WHEN CALLED BY CHRIST
When Jesus gathered the twelve disciples (Matthew 10:1–4)

■ DEATH
Judas hanged himself (Matthew 27:5; Acts 1:16–19).

■ GEOGRAPHY OF MINISTRY
Israel

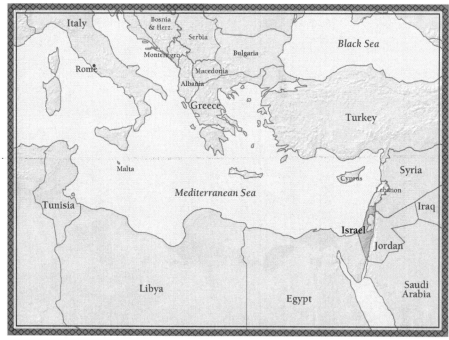

The clanging coins in the moneybag made music in Judas's ears. Not because he loved giving to the poor or providing for the disciples' needs, but because he loved money (John 12:4–6). Judas, who became a traitor, secretly helped himself to the disciples' resources without a second thought. Greed had so calcified his heart that he didn't care whom he stole from or whom he had to destroy to get his way.

Like many Jews, Judas likely hoped for a sovereign Jewish nation and expected a certain kind of Messiah—a powerful political leader who would finally end the oppressive Roman rule. Judas must've known Jesus possessed the power to be that kind of ruler; he had witnessed Jesus's miracles. Perhaps that's why Judas followed in the first place. But Jesus's talk of servitude and loving His enemies must have stirred anger and doubt in Judas. When Jesus foretold His death and even praised a woman for anointing Him for His burial, Judas drew the line. He'd waited long enough for Jesus to start acting like the Messiah. With the promise of thirty pieces of silver from the chief priests, Judas began looking for an opportunity to betray the man he had followed for three years (Matthew 26:6–16).

How could Judas—a man mentored, empowered, and groomed for leadership by Jesus Himself—have led such a double life? Judas enjoyed the advantages of friendship with the Lord as one of His closest disciples. Judas witnessed Jesus's miracles and heard His teaching daily. Jesus had even entrusted to Judas the group's money. But all those blessings produced no fruit, because greed and selfishness had spread across Judas's heart like weeds.

When Jesus commissioned the Twelve, He knew Judas would betray Him. So why did He tolerate Judas's duplicity? Because Judas had a role to play—by his own choices, Judas fulfilled Scripture by betraying the Son of Man (26:24). Jesus knew what Judas would do all along; yet until the end, Jesus loved Judas like He loved His other disciples. The One who came to serve even washed the feet of His betrayer (John 13:1–5).

Jesus invited Judas to the table in the Upper Room for His last meal. The food they shared were signs of true fellowship. But Jesus, the One who penetrates our facades and sees into our hearts, knew His betrayer from the beginning. Judas, blinded by selfish ambition, couldn't see Jesus's identity and purpose. Judas had opened himself to Satan's influence.

As Judas dipped his bread in the wine one last time with Jesus, perhaps his hand brushed the hand of the Lamb, who would soon spill His blood for the betrayer. In this moment, when Judas could have found true communion with God through repentance, the disciple hardened his heart. The Enemy's presence filled Judas and he rushed out of Jesus's presence (John 13:27).

After the traitor left the Upper Room, he went to the temple to claim his payment—thirty pieces of silver. How could Judas have handed over his intimate friend for so little? No one can know for sure, but it's possible Judas hoped Jesus would "step up" and overthrow the Romans when the temple soldiers captured Him or that Jesus's death would spark the revolution Judas had hoped for.

Whatever Judas was thinking, he forsook his commitment to Jesus and made good on his deal with the chief priests. He led the temple soldiers to Gethsemane, where at his signal—a kiss of friendship—they took Jesus captive. Judas sold his Lord to those who wanted to kill Him. The Enemy seemed to have won.

Greed always results in death—the death of contentment, joy, and fellowship with God and others. These demand selfless love. They require us to elevate the needs of others above our own (Philippians 2:3–4). Selfish ambition always leaves a path of destruction in its wake, and sometimes, the consequences seem too hard to endure. We want to take it back, make it right. But it's often too late.

Seeing that Jesus, an innocent man, had been condemned to crucifixion, Judas felt remorse. But regret doesn't indicate repentance. Regret can bring us closer to repentance, but it's not the same. Repentance requires a complete change of mind and direction. While Scripture doesn't explicitly reveal that Judas never repented—that he chose hell when he chose to betray the Messiah—Jesus's prayer in the gospel of John and Peter's prayer in Acts indicate that Judas's regret didn't lead to repentance (John 17:12; Acts 1:25). Instead, his regret led him back to the bloodthirsty men who had bought the disciple's kiss of betrayal.

But it was too late.

The chief priests and elders refused to relent and shifted the blame for Jesus's impending death onto Judas's shoulders. For once in his life, money had no appeal. He threw the silver onto the ground, and with the clanging of coins still ringing in his ears, Judas left. The bitter taste of unassuageable regret led the villain of the Gospels to the unthinkable—suicide.

The tragic life of Judas Iscariot teaches us that no one is immune to the insidious, corrosive power of secret sin, greed, and selfish ambition. Judas couldn't fool Jesus with his appearance of sincerity, and we can't fool Him with our outward piety either. The Lord knows who we are, just as He knew who Judas was. Regardless what secrets He sees in our hearts, He loves us.

The Enemy did not win when Judas betrayed the Lord. Jesus rose from the dead, and if we have confessed Him as Savior, we have assurance of salvation. But selfish ambition can still divide our hearts and our relationships. When consequences catch up with us and regret overwhelms us, it's evidence of God's grace. May such sorrow move us toward our forgiving Father.

—*Malia Rodriguez*

The Rest of the Story: Mark 14; Luke 22

TAKE IT TO HEART

What memories of regret are still ringing in your ears? Has your regret led to true repentance? Are you following Jesus because you love Him, or has selfish ambition crept into your faith?

MATTHIAS

GOD'S SURPRISE WITNESS

They prayed and said, "You, Lord, who know the hearts of all men, show which one of these two You have chosen to occupy this ministry and apostleship. . . ." And they drew lots for them, and the lot fell to Matthias; and he was added to the eleven apostles. —Acts 1:24–26

MATTHIAS

■ MEANING OF NAME
Matthias is a shortened form of Mattathias which means: "gift of God."

■ VOCATION
Unknown, though perhaps a fisherman, like the other Galileans

■ ORIGIN
Likely Galilee

■ WHEN CALLED BY CHRIST
At the beginning of Jesus's ministry, from the baptism of John

■ DEATH
"He was stoned at Jerusalem and then beheaded." [1]

■ GEOGRAPHY OF MINISTRY
Unknown

Ever since John the Baptist had prepared the way for the Messiah, Matthias had followed. He had walked in Jesus's footsteps from the Jordan River to the rugged hills of Galilee. He had followed the Savior with passion and persuasion . . . and without recognition.

Matthias was a willing unknown.

Early on, Jesus had chosen His twelve apostles from among the many disciples who shadowed Him. Even though Matthias qualified as much as any of the twelve who made the list, he wasn't selected. But that didn't matter. Matthias followed anyway. He listened with amazement to the Sermon on the Mount that day beside the Sea of Galilee. He ate his fill of fish and loaves on the Plain of Bethsaida. He witnessed the miraculous healings in Capernaum and Chorazin. He lent his voice to the throng that praised Jesus as He rode the donkey down the Mount of Olives for that final Passover with Jesus. One week later, Matthias witnessed his world turn upside down—as the One he had faithfully followed died on a Roman cross. Three days later, however, Matthias's hopes resurrected as Jesus showed Himself alive from the grave.

For more than three years, Matthias had witnessed it all—in absolute obscurity. The Gospels never mention his name; yet he was there on every page.

Now, Matthias had gathered with the apostles and many other follow-ers of Christ in an upstairs room large enough to seat the whole group of one hundred twenty. The room also held dozens of memories. Only a few weeks earlier, the Lord Jesus had reclined here at the table with His twelve disciples. They had enjoyed a final Passover meal together, as well as significant conver-sation and teaching. But then the evening fell dark and their sorrow deepened as Jesus made grave predictions of their imminent failures. They sang a hymn as they left the room and entered the night.

What came next all happened just as Jesus predicted. Peter denied the Lord, all others deserted Him, and Judas betrayed his master. The guilt-ridden traitor then tried to strangle his sorrow by hanging himself—ironically, in the same valley Jesus had used as an illustration of hell.

Jesus's glorious resurrection had given the disillusioned group of disci-ples a new hope and a new purpose—a goal beyond the personal greatness they had chased for more than three years. Jesus had commissioned His disciples to *make disciples* of all nations. As He ascended to heaven, Jesus told His many followers standing on the Mount of Olives, "You shall be My witnesses" (Acts 1:8). Matthias heard it himself. He, too, had seen Jesus ascend.

Everyone in the Upper Room that day knew Jesus had promised the *twelve* apostles they would sit on *twelve* thrones over the *twelve* tribes of Israel. Judas's vacant seat needed addressing, and soon. After all, Jesus's followers expected the promised Holy Spirit at any time. And they lived in anticipation of Jesus's imminent coming to take them to heaven before His return to rule (John 14:1–3; Acts 1:6–8).

Peter rose to his feet. There in the same room where Jesus had predicted Judas's betrayal, Peter explained, through the Holy Spirit's inspiration, Scripture's prediction that Judas would need to be replaced (Acts 1:20). The need to fill the hole he left suggested Judas had never placed his faith in Jesus (1:25)—a point that would soon be affirmed when James surrendered his head to the sword and no one saw the need to replace him. James will rise again to sit on a throne in Israel. Judas's resurrection will have a very different destiny (Revelation 20:14–15).

Peter described with precision the qualifications for serving as one of the twelve apostles:

> "Therefore it is necessary that of the men who have accompanied us all the time that the Lord Jesus went in and out among us—beginning with the baptism of John until the day that He was taken up from us—one of these must become a witness with us of His resurrection." (Acts 1:21–22)

Following a discussion, only two qualified men became clear: one named Joseph . . . and Matthias. The group prayed, and God revealed that He had chosen Matthias to serve in Judas's place as an apostle and as a witness of Jesus's resurrection.

Most likely, no one was more surprised than Matthias. The one whose name means "gift of God" became just that for the early church—God's gift of a godly leader. God's surprise witness.

Matthias never followed Jesus in order to serve as an apostle. He didn't stick around to fill the first vacancy; he never hoped to unseat the first slacker. He didn't even climb the steps to the Upper Room that day to fish for votes. Matthias simply followed Jesus from the very beginning—with no motive but faithfulness.

Repeatedly in Scripture we see individuals who began with obscure faithfulness—people like Joseph, Ruth, David, Daniel, Esther, and even Jesus—and then God expanded their influence for His glory. In each case, God alone gave the promotion.

It's the same with us. When we beg God to rescue us from our insignificant lives, believing nothing important is happening with us, Matthias reminds us that just the opposite is true. We need to see our obscurity as our significant opportunity. Faithfulness in obscurity today positions us in a place of greater influence for God tomorrow (Matthew 25:21).

Matthias never appears again in the book of Acts or anywhere else in Scripture. He emerges for a moment and then vanishes again into obscurity—a willing unknown who followed God with only the motive of faithfulness.

—*Wayne Stiles*

The Rest of the Story: Acts 1:1–26

TAKE IT TO HEART

How does Matthias's faithfulness during those years of seeming insignificance encourage you where you are right now? Do you see obscurity as your opportunity to honor an audience of one—God alone?

JAMES
THE BROTHER OF CHRIST
CALLING ALL TO LIFE

Therefore it is my judgment that we do not trouble those who are turning to God from among the Gentiles.
—*Acts 15:19*

JAMES

THE BROTHER OF CHRIST

■ MEANING OF NAME
James is the Greek version of Jacob in Hebrew, which means "supplanter."

■ VOCATION
Unknown

■ ORIGIN
Nazareth

■ WHEN CALLED BY CHRIST
Half-brother of Jesus, believed only after the resurrection

■ DEATH
Thrown down from the temple mount and stoned to death

■ GEOGRAPHY OF MINISTRY
Jerusalem

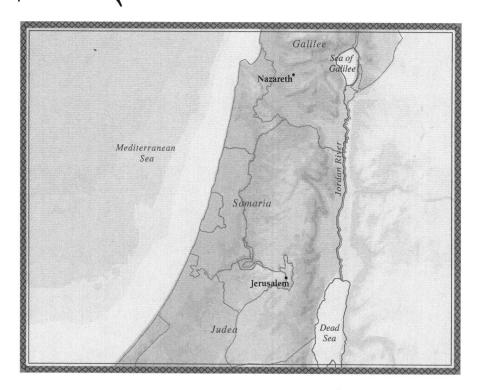

F amily breeds familiarity.

    We know the people we live with better than anyone else on earth. The rhythms of their lives and thinking are second nature to us. Often we can predict their ways of responding to situations. The closeness of our family relationships can give us an unparalleled sense of community and connection. However, when one of those family members does something out of the ordinary or strikes out on a path distinct from the rest, we often end up feeling angry, abandoned, and ashamed.

    James, one of Jesus's four half-brothers (Matthew 13:55; Mark 6:3), likely felt some combination of these negative emotions as Jesus came of age and began His ministry throughout Galilee and Judea. Sure, Jesus had been making a name for Himself. He had even gathered several disciples who traveled with Him and soaked up His teaching. But Jesus's calls for repentance (Mark 1:15) and especially His propensity to offer forgiveness of sins (2:5; 3:28) made the carpenter's son an object of judgment among the religious leaders of the day. And those who cast scorn upon Jesus wouldn't have hesitated to look down upon His family too. No family would rejoice at such difficulties.

    Therefore, when James, his mother, and his other brothers heard that Jesus had returned to His hometown—drawing a crowd and preaching to them—they hurried to Jesus, declaring Him to have "lost His senses" (3:21). Jesus would have none of their pleas to leave and disperse the crowd. He announced instead that His family was comprised only of those who do the will of God. The implication, of course, was that His family, by trying to hinder His ministry, was not doing the will of God.

    Such pronouncements within families, even from the Lord Himself, can lead to division and resentment. The apostle John recounted a story that uncovers another such chasm between Jesus and His siblings. In John's account, James and his brothers suggested to Jesus that He travel south to Judea and continue His preaching there. James and his brothers wanted Jesus to get out of town! But that's not all. A deeper layer of conflict surfaces when we consider that they made their sinister suggestion knowing that Jesus had left Judea because the Jews there had threatened His life (John 7:3–4). The story of Joseph comes to mind (Genesis 37:18–36), as James and his brothers apparently wouldn't have minded if the Jews of Judea killed Jesus. Though

Jesus resisted the devious plot, the incident revealed that His brothers were clearly not among His followers (John 7:5).

Sometime later, probably after Jesus resurrected, James came to believe that Jesus was actually who He had claimed to be. The Lord even appeared to James after the resurrection and commissioned him to apostleship (1 Corinthians 15:7). Though we have no biblical record of James's conversion, as we do for Paul, the Bible does record the spiritual fruit in James's life that attests to his following Christ.

James became a leader within the church at Jerusalem. When Paul traveled there to meet Peter for the first time, Paul met only one other apostle: James (Galatians 1:18–19). Another time, when Peter had been arrested in Jerusalem and miraculously set free by an angel, he asked those he met to let "James and the brethren" know what had happened (Acts 12:17). And as Paul completed his third missionary journey, he returned to Jerusalem, where he visited with "James, and all the elders" (21:18). The appearance of the resurrected Christ breathed new life into James, much as it did for Paul on the road to Damascus.

James's most significant moment on the biblical stage, however, happened at the Jerusalem Council, a meeting of Paul, Barnabas, Peter, James, and other early Christian leaders who came together to decide the answer to a pressing question in the ancient church: did new Gentile believers need to be circumcised?

A number of Jewish Christians believed that all Christians should seek to observe Mosaic Law (15:5). At the Jerusalem Council, Peter spoke in opposition to this group, arguing that God made no distinction between Jews and Gentiles—they had all been cleansed by faith (15:8–9). Paul and Barnabas then testified to God's working among the Gentiles.

James listened silently to the proceedings. When he stood to speak, however, everyone listened. Among this who's who of early Christian leaders, James alone made the judgment that the Gentiles need not be circumcised when they confess their faith in Jesus. God had always meant to bring Gentiles into His kingdom, as the prophets had testified. Jewish Christians, then, had no business making the Gentiles' assimilation into the community more difficult than it already was (Acts 15:13–21).

James underwent a radical transformation. Early in his life, he chose to keep his distance from Jesus, even to the point of being willing to send the Lord away to His death. However, late in life, James clung to Jesus like a true brother, following Him in both word and deed. This changed perspective rings clear in the one epistle James wrote. He who had once sought to undermine Jesus came to consider himself "a bond-servant of God and of the Lord Jesus Christ" (James 1:1).

What did that mean for James? The same as it should mean for all who believe—committing to life in its fullness from the moment of conversion forward. Until his own death, James faithfully preached Jesus resurrected from the dead. Under the apostle's ministry and through his inspired writing, millions of people of *all* kinds—Jews and Gentiles alike—have been presented with the opportunity to embrace that message in word and deed, join God's family, and receive the inheritance of eternal life.

—John Adair

The Rest of the Story: John 7:3–5; Acts 15:1–35

TAKE IT TO HEART

Do you ever find yourself in James's shoes of resisting Jesus's teaching because it seems too radical? How so? How does James's willingness to make the offer of salvation to the Gentiles help you understand grace?

PAUL
BROUGHT DOWN
TO BUILD THE CHURCH

For I neither received [the gospel] from man, nor was I taught it, but I received it through a revelation of Jesus Christ. —Galatians 1:12

PAUL

■ MEANING OF NAME
The name Saul means "the asked for one." The name Paul means "small."

■ VOCATION
Tent maker

■ ORIGIN
Tarsus

■ WHEN CALLED BY CHRIST
While on a trip to Damascus to persecute Christians (Acts 9)

■ DEATH
"The soldiers came and led him out of the city to the place of execution, where he, after his prayers made, gave his neck to the sword." [1]

■ GEOGRAPHY OF MINISTRY
Israel, Syria, Cyprus, Asia Minor (modern-day Turkey), Macedonia, Greece, Italy, Spain, and Gaul (modern-day France)

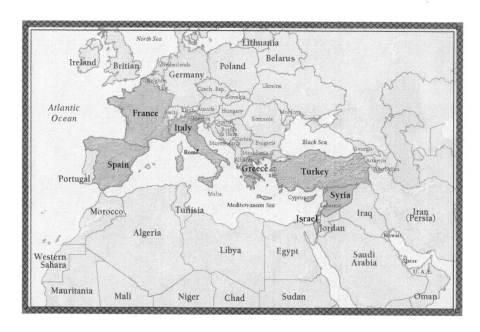

With crossed arms and questioning eyes, they stared at him. Could they really trust him? The Christians in Damascus and Jerusalem struggled to believe his story of a bright light and a booming voice from heaven (Acts 9:19–21, 26). The man who stood before them had been a persecutor of Christians. That was his job. With every breath, Saul had inhaled hatred for Jesus and His followers and exhaled death threats. The Jewish high priest, having recognized Saul's fanaticism, had given him permission to bind believers in Damascus and bring them to Jerusalem to face death (9:1–2). But something happened on his way to Damascus to turn this professional terrorist into a follower of Jesus.

But how did Saul get to a place where he could become a professional terrorist in the first place?

Born into the tribe of Benjamin, a purebred Hebrew and member of the Pharisees, Saul had complete confidence that he was on God's side. Saul had grown up memorizing the Torah and learning how to live as a virtuous Jew. As a young man, he had studied under Gamaliel, a prominent and respected rabbi, and excelled among the Pharisees (22:3). Saul even considered himself totally righteous—*flawless* when it came to obeying the Jewish Law (Philippians 3:5–6).

Somewhere along Saul's "righteous" way, though, pride took over. Saul's self-righteousness and zeal must have taken over and, in his mind, Saul became judge and jury, proclaiming some righteous and some worthy of death. Saul even went on missions to foreign cities to hunt down those who did not measure up—those who followed Jesus (Acts 26:9–11).

But on one of Saul's foreign missions, his direction changed. As Saul journeyed to Damascus to terrorize Christians, Jesus knocked Saul off his feet and leveled his pride (9:1–30). The resurrected Messiah called out, "Saul, Saul, why are you persecuting Me?" (9:4). Physically blinded by the flashing light from heaven, Saul realized he hadn't seen anything clearly. Although he thought he was rightfully punishing misguided Christians, really he was battling the true Messiah. In the middle of Saul's journey to destroy the name of Christ, Jesus Himself intervened. Saul changed. And so did history.

Jesus appointed Saul, who came to be known by his Roman name Paul, as His apostle to the Gentiles (Acts 9:15; 1 Corinthians 15:8). And for the rest of Paul's life, the Lord and His calling consumed the apostle's heart, mind, soul, and strength. He fearlessly told Gentiles about God's grace, and he willingly endured the path of sacrifice that God had set out for him.

And sacrifice he did. After years of fruitful ministry to the Gentiles, Jewish authorities brought charges against Paul and tried to kill him (Acts 23:12–15). Their harassment had so escalated that the Roman official who guarded Paul worried the Jews would tear him apart (23:10). After a grueling day of defending himself, Paul collapsed in bed. In the middle of the night, Jesus appeared and said, "Be encouraged, Paul. Just as you have been a witness to me here in Jerusalem, you must preach the Good News in Rome as well" (23:11 NLT). The tables of persecution had turned. But in the midst of the suffering that now burdened Paul, the Lord spoke to him and gave him courage, equipping him for the difficult ministry God had given him.

Before Paul made it to Rome, he faced King Agrippa and a trial for teaching Jesus as Israel's true Messiah, the One Moses and the prophets foretold (26:6–7). And throughout his ministry, Paul endured imprisonments, floggings, lashings, stonings, shipwrecks, exhaustion, hunger, poverty, and ultimately death by beheading (2 Corinthians 11:22–28). The pain he endured proved the sincerity of his faith.

God took this man who had instilled widespread terror in the hearts of believers and used him to spread the gospel of peace farther than anyone could've imagined. Paul helped build the Christian church throughout Asia and Greece, pushing the gospel westward, encouraging persecuted believers, advocating for the truth, and bringing Gentiles to saving faith in a way still unrivaled among believers. The testimony of his missionary journeys and his letters to fellow believers and young Christian churches make up a large portion of the New Testament. Through Paul's pen, God explained the truth of His gospel and the mystery of salvation like never before.

Paul's interactions with Jesus completely changed him. The man who once bowed to human opinion came to live his life prostrate before Christ (Galatians 1:10). All the accolades that once motivated him completely lost their appeal. When Jesus appeared to Paul, grabbed his heart, and redirected his life, Paul left everything behind, declaring, "Yes, everything else is worthless when compared with the infinite value of knowing Christ Jesus my Lord. For his sake I have discarded everything else, counting it all as garbage, so that I could gain Christ" (Philippians 3:8 NLT).

Paul's training in Jewish Law and Old Testament theology and his passionate personality formed lines that converged at the cross. There, Jesus harnessed Paul's zeal and used his past to point others to God's transforming power.

Many of us have been Christ followers for so long we hardly remember what it was like to live without Him. For others, Christ captured our hearts later, and we remember life without Him like it was yesterday. Either way, if we have confessed Christ and dedicated ourselves to being His disciples, Jesus has changed our lives. All believers have received a calling from the Lord, and often we discover that calling at the intersection of our most fervent passions and our most profound pains. Whether we have drastic testimonies like Paul's or "ordinary" stories, God's work to transform us from desperate sinners to righteous saints is dramatic. And He will use our stories to bring people to Him — if we truly consider the lures of this world as filthy, stinking garbage. Paul did . . . and it changed his life, and the world, forever.

—*Malia Rodriguez*

The Rest of the Story: Galatians 1:13–24; Philippians 3:7–11

TAKE IT TO HEART

How has Jesus transformed your character, goals, and relationships? How has the Lord used your past to minister to others and to bring glory to Him? What are some creative ways you can combine your pain and your passion to help others?

AFTERWORD FROM CHUCK

Centuries of stained glass have colored our view of the apostles. We see these men as bold, larger-than-life heroes who journeyed the world for Christ and paid the ultimate price for their faith.

Men of God. Missionaries. Models. Martyrs.

It's easy to forget they were really just ordinary people. Self-assured, self-confident fishermen, who left their nets and followed Jesus even though they often didn't understand Him. Young, passionate men who waffled between arguing about who among them was the greatest . . . and expressing to Jesus their willingness to die for Him. Frail and fearful men who ran like rabbits when their Lord was arrested in Gethsemane.

Ordinary people . . . who took extraordinary adventures.

We live in strange times where the great goal of life is retirement. I've looked, but I can't find *retirement* anywhere in the Bible. Now, there's nothing wrong per se with leaving the workforce at a certain age. But to retire from life with the mind-set, "I've paid my dues, so leave me alone! I now plan to do what I want"? There's none of that attitude in Scripture. In fact, we see quite the opposite.

Personally, I never plan to retire. In fact, I hope to die in the pulpit right after I say, "Amen." (I'd like my chin to hit the podium on the way down.) Doing what God has called us to do until the last possible moment—that's what I find when I read the book of Acts! I would love it if we called *The Acts of the Apostles* by another name, like: *The Adventures of the Apostles*. Wouldn't that be good?

Life for a follower of Christ is an adventure. I'm not talking about non-sensible adventures, like building a house at the base of Mt. Vesuvius or hang gliding over the Devil's Triangle. I don't mean doing something dumb and irresponsible. I'm referring to getting out of our little world.

You see, that's what the Lord Jesus had in mind when He set forth His plan for these frightened, intimidated fishermen. *The Adventures of the Apostles* begins with Jesus's final words on earth, delivered to a group of ordinary people:

> "You will receive power when the Holy Spirit comes upon you. And you will be my witnesses, telling people about me everywhere—in Jerusalem, throughout Judea, in Samaria, and to the ends of the earth." (Acts 1:8 NLT)

Jesus promised His disciples power as He gave them their marching orders: "You will be My witnesses." What are witnesses? They're simply people who tell other people what they saw or experienced. Witnesses are people who tell the truth about what has happened in their lives.

The Lord Jesus intended His disciples to have engaging, contagious lifestyles. Per His direction, they began in Jerusalem, and as the Holy Spirit led them, their influence expanded to include the far-reaching regions of the earth . . . including, eventually, you and me. It *still* includes you and me, by the way.

Say . . . *what about you?*

I urge you to begin engaging your "Jerusalem." Be His witness! Where is your Jerusalem? It's where you live . . . your home base. Dallas, San Diego, Miami, Baltimore, Boston—wherever it is, start right there. Begin at your school . . . your office . . . your club . . . your job. Wherever you go each day, make that your Jerusalem.

The assignment Jesus gave His disciples is still in effect. (We know because He hasn't returned for us yet.) The first disciples followed His command, and God used them to turn the world "upside down." They made a lasting difference. He'll do the same with us.

After all, we're all just ordinary people.

—Chuck

HOW TO BEGIN A RELATIONSHIP WITH GOD

Success and failure mark our lives. Thankfully, God included in His Word *real* stories of *real* people—complete with their shortcomings—to encourage us and point us to our need for the mercy of the one and only perfect God. The apostles were no different than the rest of us. Like us, before they met Jesus, they were sinners in desperate need of restoration with God. God's solution for all humankind unfolded before the apostles' eyes. Jesus Christ changed their lives on earth and breathed eternal life into their souls. He can do the same for you. From Genesis to Revelation, God's Word reveals four essential truths we must accept and apply to find the life-transforming remedy He offers. Let's look at these four truths in detail.

OUR SPIRITUAL CONDITION: TOTALLY DEPRAVED

The first truth is rather personal. One look in the mirror of Scripture, and our human condition becomes painfully clear:

> "There is none righteous, not even one;
> There is none who understands,
> There is none who seeks for God;
> All have turned aside, together they have become useless;
> There is none who does good,
> There is not even one." (Romans 3:10–12)

We are all sinners through and through—totally depraved. Now, that doesn't mean we've committed every atrocity known to humankind. We're not as *bad* as we can be, just as *bad off* as we can be. Sin colors all our thoughts, motives, words, and actions.

If you've been around a while, you likely already believe it. Look around. Everything around us bears the smudge marks of our sinful nature. Despite our best efforts to create a perfect world, crime statistics continue to soar, divorce rates keep climbing, and families keep crumbling.

Something has gone terribly wrong in our society and in ourselves—something deadly. Contrary to how the world would repackage it, "me-first" living doesn't equal rugged individuality and freedom; it equals death. As Paul said in his letter to the Romans, "The wages of sin is death" (Romans 6:23)—our spiritual and physical death that comes from God's righteous judgment of our sin, along with all of the emotional and practical effects of this separation that we experience on a daily basis. This brings us to the second marker: God's character.

GOD'S CHARACTER: INFINITELY HOLY

How can God judge us for a sinful state we were born into? Our total depravity is only half the answer. The other half is God's infinite holiness.

The fact that we know things are not as they should be points us to a standard of goodness beyond ourselves. Our sense of injustice in life on this side of eternity implies a perfect standard of justice beyond our reality. That standard and source is God Himself. And God's standard of holiness contrasts starkly with our sinful condition.

Scripture says that "God is Light, and in Him there is no darkness at all" (1 John 1:5). God is absolutely holy—which creates a problem for us. If He is so pure, how can we who are so impure relate to Him?

Perhaps we could try being better people, try to tilt the balance in favor of our good deeds, or seek out methods for self-improvement. Throughout history, people have attempted to live up to God's standard by keeping the Ten Commandments or living by their own code of ethics. Unfortunately, no one can come close to satisfying the demands of God's Law. Romans 3:20 says, "By the works of the Law no flesh will be justified in His sight; for through the Law comes the knowledge of sin."

OUR NEED: A SUBSTITUTE

So here we are, sinners by nature and sinners by choice, trying to pull ourselves up by our own bootstraps to attain a relationship with our holy Creator. But every time we try, we fall flat on our faces. We can't live a good enough life to make up for our sin, because God's standard isn't "good enough"—it's *perfection*. And we can't make amends for the offense our sin has created without dying for it.

Who can get us out of this mess?

If someone could live perfectly, honoring God's Law, and would bear sin's death penalty for us—in our place—then we would be saved from our predicament. But is there such a person? Thankfully, yes!

Meet your substitute—*Jesus Christ*. He is the One who took death's place for you!

> [God] made [Jesus Christ] who knew no sin to be sin on our behalf, so that we might become the righteousness of God in Him. (2 Corinthians 5:21)

GOD'S PROVISION: A SAVIOR

God rescued us by sending His Son, Jesus, to die on the cross for our sins (1 John 4:9–10). Jesus was fully human and fully divine (John 1:1, 18), a truth that ensures His understanding of our weaknesses, His power to forgive, and His ability to bridge the gap between God and us (Romans 5:6–11). In short, we are "justified as a gift by His grace through the redemption which is in Christ Jesus" (Romans 3:24). Two words in this verse bear further explanation: *justified* and *redemption*.

Justification is God's act of mercy, in which He declares righteous the believing sinners while we are still in our sinning state. Justification doesn't mean that God *makes* us righteous, so that we never sin again, rather that He *declares* us righteous—much like a judge pardons a guilty criminal. Because Jesus took our sin upon Himself and suffered our judgment on the cross, God forgives our debt and proclaims us PARDONED.

Redemption is Christ's act of paying the complete price to release us from sin's bondage. God sent His Son to bear His wrath for all of our sins—past, present, and future (Romans 3:24–26; 2 Corinthians 5:21). In humble obedience, Christ willingly endured the shame of the cross for our sake (Mark 10:45; Romans 5:6–8; Philippians 2:8). Christ's death satisfied God's righteous demands. He no longer holds our sins against us, because His own Son paid the penalty for them. We are freed from the slave market of sin, never to be enslaved again!

PLACING YOUR FAITH IN CHRIST

These four truths describe how God has provided a way to Himself through Jesus Christ. Because the price has been paid in full by God, we must respond to His free gift of eternal life in total faith and confidence in Him to save us. We must step forward into the relationship with God that He has prepared for us — not by doing good works or by being a good person, but by coming to Him just as we are and accepting His justification and redemption by faith.

> For by grace you have been saved through faith; and that not of yourselves, it is the gift of God; not as a result of works, so that no one may boast. (Ephesians 2:8–9)

We accept God's gift of salvation simply by placing our faith in Christ alone for the forgiveness of our sins. Would you like to enter a relationship with your Creator by trusting in Christ as your Savior? If so, here's a simple prayer you can use to express your faith:

> *Dear God,*
>
> *I know that my sin has put a barrier between You and me. Thank You for sending Your Son, Jesus, to die in my place. I trust in Jesus alone to forgive my sins, and I accept His gift of eternal life. I ask Jesus to be my personal Savior and the Lord of my life. Thank You. In Jesus's name, amen.*

If you've prayed this prayer or one like it and you wish to find out more about knowing God and His plan for you in the Bible, contact us at Insight for Living Ministries. Our contact information is provided on the following pages.

WE ARE HERE FOR YOU

I f you desire to find out more about knowing God and His plan for you in the Bible, contact us. Insight for Living Ministries provides staff pastors who are available for free written correspondence or phone consultation. These seminary-trained and seasoned counselors have years of experience and are well-qualified guides for your spiritual journey.

Please feel welcome to contact your regional office by using the information below.

United States

Insight for Living Ministries
Biblical Counseling Department
Post Office Box 5000
Frisco, Texas 75034-0055
USA
972-473-5097 (Monday through Friday,
8:00 a.m. – 5:00 p.m. central time)
www.insight.org/contactapastor

Canada

Insight for Living Canada
Biblical Counseling Department
PO Box 8 Stn A
Abbotsford BC V2T 6Z4
CANADA
1-800-663-7639
info@insightforliving.ca

Australia, New Zealand, and South Pacific

Insight for Living Australia
Pastoral Care
Post Office Box 443
Boronia, VIC 3155
AUSTRALIA
1300 467 444

United Kingdom and Europe

Insight for Living United Kingdom
Pastoral Care
PO Box 553
Dorking
RH4 9EU
UNITED KINGDOM
0800 787 9364
+44 (0)1306 640156
pastoralcare@insightforliving.org.uk

ENDNOTES

ANDREW

1. *Fox's Book of Martyrs: A History of the Lives, Sufferings and Deaths of the Early Christian and Protestant Martyrs*, ed. William Byron Forbush (Grand Rapids: Zondervan, 1967), 3. (Accessed on Google Books, Sept. 5, 2013.)

PHILIP

1. *Fox's Book of Martyrs: A History of the Lives, Sufferings and Deaths of the Early Christian and Protestant Martyrs*, ed. William Byron Forbush (Grand Rapids: Zondervan, 1967), 3. (Accessed on Google Books, Sept. 5, 2013.)

2. E. A. Wallis Budge, *The Contendings of the Apostles*, vol. 2 (New York: Oxford University Press, 1901),156–62, http://archive.org/stream/contendingsofapo02budguoft#page/n7/mode/2up, accessed Aug. 27, 2013.

NATHANAEL

1. V. R. Gordon, "Nathanael," in *The International Standard Bible Encyclopedia*, vol. 3, *K–P*, rev. ed., ed. Geoffrey W. Bromiley and others (Grand Rapids: Eerdmans, 1987), 491–92.

2. *Fox's Book of Martyrs: A History of the Lives, Sufferings and Deaths of the Early Christian and Protestant Martyrs*, ed. William Byron Forbush (Grand Rapids: Zondervan, 1967), 4. (Accessed on Google Books, Sept. 5, 2013.)

3. Merrill F. Unger, "Nazareth," in *The New Unger's Bible Dictionary*, ed. R. K. Harrison (Chicago: Moody Press, 1988), 907.

JAMES THE SON OF ALPHAEUS

1. *Fox's Book of Martyrs: A History of the Lives, Sufferings and Deaths of the Early Christian and Protestant Martyrs*, ed. William Byron Forbush (Grand Rapids: Zondervan, 1967), 3. (Accessed on Google Books, Sept. 5, 2013.)

2. E. A. Wallis Budge, *The Contendings of the Apostles*, vol. 2 (New York: Oxford University Press, 1901), 264–66, http://archive.org/stream/contendingsofapo02budguoft#page/n7/mode/2up, accessed Aug. 27, 2013.

SIMON THE ZEALOT

1. *Fox's Book of Martyrs: A History of the Lives, Sufferings and Deaths of the Early Christian and Protestant Martyrs*, ed. William Byron Forbush (Grand Rapids: Zondervan, 1967), 5. (Accessed on Google Books, Sept. 5, 2013.)

2. Louis A. Barbieri, Jr., "Matthew," in *The Bible Knowledge Commentary: New Testament*, ed. John F. Walvoord and Roy B. Zuck (Wheaton, Ill.: Victor, 1989), 41.

MATTHIAS

1. *Fox's Book of Martyrs: A History of the Lives, Sufferings and Deaths of the Early Christian and Protestant Martyrs*, ed. William Byron Forbush (Grand Rapids: Zondervan, 1967), 3. (Accessed on Google Books, Sept. 5, 2013.)

PAUL

1. *Fox's Book of Martyrs: A History of the Lives, Sufferings and Deaths of the Early Christian and Protestant Martyrs*, ed. William Byron Forbush (Grand Rapids: Zondervan, 1967), 4. (Accessed on Google Books, Sept. 5, 2013.)

RESOURCES FOR PROBING FURTHER

The lives of Jesus's apostles display fear, faith, betrayal, and belief. But Jesus used these men, with all their faults, to build His church. And He can do the same with you. We have compiled a list of resources that will help you dig deeper into the stories and lessons behind these disciples' lives. We hope you will use them to draw closer to our Savior and to gain His wisdom for each new day. Keep in mind as you read these that we can't always endorse everything a writer or ministry says, so we encourage you to approach with wisdom and discernment these and all other non-biblical resources.

Bridges, Jerry. *The Pursuit of Holiness*. Colorado Springs: NavPress, 2006.

Bruce, A. B. *The Training of the Twelve: Timeless Principles for Leadership Development*. Grand Rapids: Kregel Publications, 2000.

Insight for Living. *Adventuring with God: Following in the Apostles' Footsteps*. Plano, Tex.: IFL Publishing House, 2002.

Insight for Living. *One-on-One Discipleship: Ministry Up-Close and Personal*. Anaheim, Calif.: Insight for Living, 1999.

Insight for Living. *Practical Christian Living: A Road Map to Spiritual Growth*. Plano, Tex.: IFL Publishing House, 2008.

Swindoll, Charles R. *Growing Deep in the Christian Life: Essential Truths for Becoming Strong in the Faith*. Grand Rapids: Zondervan, 1995.

Swindoll, Charles R. *Jesus: The Greatest Life of All*. Great Lives Series. Nashville: Thomas Nelson, 2008.

Swindoll, Charles R. *Paul: A Man of Grace and Grit*. Great Lives Series. Nashville: Thomas Nelson, 2009.

Walvoord, John F., and Roy B. Zuck, eds. *The Bible Knowledge Commentary: An Exposition of the Scriptures by Dallas Seminary Faculty, New Testament Edition*. Wheaton, Ill.: Victor Books, 1989.

ORDERING INFORMATION

If you would like to order additional copies of *Shaping the Modern Disciple: Lessons from Jesus's Apostles* or other Insight for Living Ministries resources, please contact the office that serves you.

United States

Insight for Living Ministries
Post Office Box 5000
Frisco, Texas 75034-0055
USA
1-800-772-8888
(Monday through Friday, 7:00 a.m.–7:00 p.m. central time)
www.insight.org
www.insightworld.org

Canada

Insight for Living Canada
PO Box 8 Stn A
Abbotsford BC V2T 6Z4
CANADA
1-800-663-7639
www.insightforliving.ca

Australia, New Zealand, and South Pacific

Insight for Living Australia
Post Office Box 443
Boronia, VIC 3155
AUSTRALIA
1300 467 444
www.insight.asn.au

Ordering Information

United Kingdom and Europe

Insight for Living United Kingdom
PO Box 553
Dorking
RH4 9EU
UNITED KINGDOM
0800 787 9364
www.insightforliving.org.uk

Other International Locations

International constituents may contact the U.S. office through our Web site (www.insightworld.org), mail queries, or by calling +1-972-473-5136.